SON OF THE CALI CARTEL

THE NARCOS WHO WIPED OUT PABLO ESCOBAR AND THE MEDELLÍN CARTEL

WILLIAM RODRÍGUEZ ABADÍA

CHAPTER 1

"They killed him! They killed him!"

When I heard my aunt's voice, I felt joy. *I'm OK,* I thought. My aunt had gone outside to make a phone call. Even though I was hurt, and I knew that I was dying, I felt at peace. It was a sort of trance produced by the loss of blood. As I felt the life slipping out of my body, I heard a voice that told me I would make it; hearing it filled me with enough strength to get up off the floor. My left knee failed me; it was fractured. I fell, and as I was about to hit the floor, I pictured my daughter. I prayed to God so he would save me. "It's not fair, Father, my daughter is only two years old!" I exclaimed. In that moment, I heard my cousin's voice, and it felt like a miracle, an answer to my prayers.

"He's alive! He's alive!"

My aunt, her face filled with anguish, came close and said, "Mijo, how are you feeling? You're alive! Thank God!"

"Call an ambulance," I told her. "Please, get an ambulance!"

Again, she ran to her phone and dialed desperately as I tried to look around at the horrifying spectacle that this crowded restaurant had turned into. Blood, death, pain, fear, anguish: all elements of the hell I found myself in and that, from this moment on, I was determined to escape.

"Take me downstairs, now! I'm going to bleed out!" I shouted.

"We don't want them to come back to finish the job!" answered one of the waiters.

I didn't care if they came back for me; I wanted to save myself. I had to do something to preserve what little life I had left in me.

"Take me down!" I told him.

The waiter hesitated for a second, but looking at the anger on my face, he realized he had no other option. When I was on the sidewalk, as I prayed for the arrival of the ambulance, two policemen arrived on a motorcycle. Immediately, I felt a stinging fear that the hired killers, to make sure that they had completed their mission, had sent these agents to finish the job. That was how these groups operated.

"Come here, brother. My name is William Rodríguez Abadia. Please don't move from my side!" I told one of the police officers that got off the bike.

The uniformed man took his time, looked at me, smiled, and said, "Don't worry about it, boss, I'm staying right here!"

I had never felt so relieved. I was always surrounded by body-guards, hired guns, and men willing to do anything to save me, and now it was a policeman who, paradoxically, was bringing me momentary relief, which let me flash back to how it all went down.

It was Friday, March 24, 1996, a day that would mark my life and that would trigger a change that, surely, my subconscious mind had prayed for. I had been born in a household led by my uncle, who, to my knowledge, was an honorable businessman. For many years, I remained unaware of my uncle's true occupation, aided by my father Miguel, which is why I grew up thinking that wealth was something normal—even though they had always told us that in order to achieve anything, one had to earn it.

I started to question the true nature of their double lives when I was a teenager. We were always surrounded by bodyguards, and people always made comments that, eventually, started filling my head with doubts ... doubts that were however soon calmed by undeniable truths: "This is my family," "This is my father," "This is my uncle," "All we really have in the world is family."

But the most powerful and influential argument against believing all of this was the comfort that having money brings. In my case, due to certain situations I had faced as a child, which I will later explain, my conscience had been easily bought. Instead of continuing to ask myself these questions, I followed the custom in the Rodríguez family, led by my uncle, who reminded us every time he could that: money can buy anything.

Once I understood this way of thinking, I dedicated myself to living my life like the son of any wealthy man, trying not to call any attention to myself so that I could continue to live a normal life as a student and a teenager.

I have always been a man that has been close to God. His light has protected me on numerous occasions, saving me from death more than once. This is why I worship a miraculous Christ, that has his home in Buga, a municipality close to Cali. That Friday, I was supposed to go to the Church in Buga with my childhood friend, Oscar Echeverri.

As I had asked, Oscar got to my house quite early. We left after breakfast, unaware that, at that same time, on the opposite end of Cali, they were putting the finishing touches on a couple of white vans, made to look exactly like those used by police. Inside of these vans, there were six men, all armed with 7.65mm pistols with silencers, and equipped with radios, who were getting ready to carry out one of the biggest assassination attempts in the city of Cali's history.

At this time, I was in charge of moderating relationships with different groups of drug-traffickers that were fighting, naively, to take control of the business. I had taken on this role at my father's request. Backed by the leader of the paramilitary forces of Colombia, the AUC, they had murdered José "Chepe" Santacruz Londoño, one of the four leaders of the Cali Cartel, and they feared our retaliation. Because of this, I had to organize various meetings, attempting to mediate and resolve conflicts due to malicious rumors that had been started by Wilber Alirio Varela, alias "Jabon," a killer that had gained the trust of Orlando Henao, the leader of the biggest cartel at the time, the North Valley Cartel (Cartel del Norte del Valle).

Oscar, along with my wife and I, were getting ready to set out for Buga as we finished breakfast. After giving the last couple of spoonfuls of compote to my daughter, I got a call from my aunt Amparo. She needed me at the headquarters of America de Cali, immediately.

My aunt Amparo, a woman with great entrepreneurial

potential, was in charge of the administrative side of things in the corporation. I was responsible for the athletics and the teams, as had been decided by my father; soccer was a passion that my father had passed on to me as a kid. Don Miguel Rodríguez loved the red shirt of América de Cali more than anything, and, in one form or another, it explained his life's philosophy.

América de Cali represented the people; it was the voice of those that had nothing, the champion of the displaced. The influence of my father on Colombian soccer lasted from 1980 until the time he lost his freedom.

It was always mentioned, in bad faith, that we had used the team to launder money. Nothing could be further from the truth. We were moved by a certain passion known as "la mechita." Something that is tattooed in our hearts. Plus, it helped me deal with the frustration I felt over never having been able to go pro in soccer, a dream that I had had since I was a child, while watching my idols like Diego Armando Maradona and Johan Cruyff.

I have always been excessively obsessive in everything I have ever done. I got that from my father, who told me over and over that, "The world did not belong to those who are mediocre." That maxim is extremely evident when it comes to soccer, a sport where "winning isn't everything, it's the only thing." And that's how it is. In soccer, no one ever remembers who came in second. Because of this, I had accepted the mission of turning this team into champions, carefully examining every single strategy and way of playing of all European teams, especially those from Holland, Italy, and Spain. I wanted América to be the best team in the world: not only for personal satisfaction, but to show my father and the rest of my family that I could do whatever they asked of me.

In response to my aunt's phone call, I headed straight to the team's headquarters, accompanied by my friend, Oscar Echeverri. Located in a remote neighborhood in Cali, quite close to Estación Avenue, América's headquarters was made up of a building with two floors, with spacious inner patios that gave it an airy feeling. As soon as I got there, I headed straight to the second floor, where my aunt was waiting for me. The meeting had to do with a negotiation with the Portuguese team Porto, that wanted to buy Jorge Hernan "Calarca" Bermudez, a Colombian soccer player who played as a defender, not only on our team, but also for the national team, and who was then at his best professionally. After this meeting was over, we had another meeting with the president of the association and the other directors to discuss some pending business regarding the professional team.

When I was finally finished, I invited my cousin Mauricio and Nicol Parra, my friend since school, to eat at a nearby restaurant called "El Rodizio." Nicol, who had, in a twist of fate, ended up being the man in charge of my father's security detail in the war with Pablo Escobar, had always kept me updated on anything that was going on in that war, which, one way or another, affected my entire family.

Nicol, El Gordo Oscar, and I agreed to meet. I asked Gordo to call Juan Carlos Delgado, an ex-lieutenant that had retired from the military, who had also worked for my father but now worked for me. Juan Carlos helped a lot when I was in Bogotá lobbying congressmen at my father's request. He was a loyal man; we became good friends after having been through difficult times together.

Nicol handed me the phone so I could convince him to come to the restaurant. Juan Carlos was with his girlfriend at that moment, a fact that would haunt my conscience for a long time. That day, I had forced him, unintentionally, to go to his death. When he suggested that we meet up later, since it was Friday and I wanted to spend a nice evening with my friends, I promptly changed my tone of voice from a cordial invitation to ordering him to show up, to accompany me as a driver and a weaponless bodyguard, due to the laws imposed by Cali's mayor, Mauricio Guzmán Cuevas, that suspended the ability to carry firearms in an attempt to reduce the violence in the city.

We were getting ready to leave the headquarters with no clue as to the fate that awaited us. My cousin Mauricio got a call that kept him from joining us, so we said goodbye right then and there.

I will never forget that, as we were leaving the building, I noticed a man on a motorcycle that stared directly at me and sped off. That "campanero," or lookout, was just the tip of the iceberg. The base was the rest of the operation that was slowly developing militarily to carry out an attack like the one that was waiting for me. This operation included having detailed city plans, escape routes, and, if it became necessary, enough ammo in case a violent confrontation ensued.

Their mission was to take us by surprise. To do this, they needed to move according to our movements, which is why their communication and their tracking had to be impeccable. The plan consisted of killing us so they could weaken my family militarily and politically: the same strategy that, at one point, had been used by Pablo Escobar in the war between the Cali Cartel and the Medellín Cartel.

These were not great moments for my family. The two heads of our family were behind bars, which left us vulnerable and at the mercy of those violent winds that blew south from the North Valley Cartel.

It was also not easy to lead a normal life. Having our last name, Rodríguez, had, in times of prosperity, brought me power and friends, but, at the first sign of trouble, these friends ran to hide behind their paper houses, pointing their finger accusingly at those that had been there for them. That was a great lesson that life taught me: it helped me realize that power and wealth are fleeting.

But, during this particular time, I did not see things that way. I felt like I was on top of the world; my ego was inflated because I had what most men want: power and recognition. At some point, I even started believing, mistakenly, that I was some kind of superhuman man that could do anything and, tragically, believed I was immortal, immune to anything—a belief that would lead me to make the worst mistakes of my life, as also did my uncle and father for believing they were untouchable. I never thought that day would come, but death always comes, suddenly and with no exceptions.

Once we were in the restaurant, we sat at a rectangular table ready to delight ourselves with some delicious meat. We were eating and chatting cheerfully. Due to pure coincidence, my aunt Amparo, her two daughters, and her sister-in-law, Ana Milena—who worked as an advisor at América de Cali—were eating at the same place. Thankfully, they were sitting at another table, close enough to exchange looks with one another that made us feel safe.

As we enjoyed our lunch, time passed with discussion of trivialities and the sharing of anecdotes about our lives that, when we looked back, had completely changed. We laughed a lot, aided by the comments made about how great our beloved team had been doing.

In one of those moments when the pleasurable sensation created by laughter is dulled by the reality around you, I noticed four men that were doing exactly what we were doing a couple of tables away, in the opposite direction of my aunt's table. They seemed to be eating lunch and, once in a while, they would all gaze at our table trying to recognize one of our men, or so I thought.

It was an instant, a moment, an eternity; I guess you never really know for sure. Suddenly, a voice or a noise would take me away from my train of thought, which could have been the clear path forged by intuition; the path that could have meant salvation for all of us had I not faltered, had I not thought that I was making a big deal out of nothing. The way that they were dressed, the blue shoes that one of them was wearing, and the fact that they seemed to be ordering food, calmed my suspicions, and I went back to sharing laughs and enjoying the meat that, according to my friends, tasted better than ever.

As I sat there, eating the meat that had been cooked perfectly, the two vans carrying the six men arrived at the door and identified themselves as members of the National Police. Having thoroughly examined their identifications, my men put up no resistance at all and, when the killers were sure that none of them were armed, they shot them all at point-blank range. They used 9mm guns with silencers, which prevented us, engulfed in laughter, from hearing the guns go off.

It was 1.55 p.m., the exact time that I made the last call before the attack. I called my wife, wanting to know if her and my precious daughter had eaten lunch; she told me that the compote from that morning had made my daughter feel sick. She gave me good news: the two loves of my life were perfectly fine, which led me to say, without knowing why, "I love you both. Take care of my daughter."

"Is something wrong, my love?" my wife wondered aloud, maybe a little surprised at the comment I had made.

I responded by saying that I simply wanted to hear her voice. "Remember that you are always in my heart."

My wife, understanding and loving, as always, said goodbye with a, "I will see you later," a moment that never came. As soon as I hung up, as if it had been perfectly timed, the four men sitting at the table opposite from us, who had seemed suspicious to me, stood up, got their weapons out, and shouted, "Everybody stay still! Nobody move!"

In that moment, I thought they were there to kidnap me.

Two of them stayed back, watching the backs of the executioners; the other two came closer, and one of them shouted, "There he is! The motherfucker in the white!"

I was not wearing white. I was wearing green. The one in white was Nicol.

That was the excuse that the leaders of the North Valley Cartel would use to justify their actions, saying that it had been a mistake, that I was not supposed to be there. But it was impossible that they had been unaware; they had been trailing us since we left the headquarters.

The strategy of this new cartel, which was beginning to exert their power as the biggest cartel in Colombia and was led by Orlando Henao and Efrain Hernández, alias "Don Efra," was to weaken us, murdering the heads of security for both my uncle and my father. Some evidence to back up this statement is that the day before my assassination attempt, they had killed Edgar Veloza, alias "El Mono," the man in charge of handling my uncle's security detail in the war with Pablo Escobar.

Criminal organizations exist and are able to work in the shadows because they have men willing to follow orders without asking why, which is also how armies work. Nicol was not an exception. He was one of the men that knew and led our military apparatus, and because of this, had been responsible for sparing and taking lives in exchange for money.

Any organization can grow strong when it has a fast response time, and, for that, men like Nicol are needed in the ranks, who are willing to put an end to anyone and anything to prove their loyalty to their boss. This is why the top priority that day had been to kill Nicol.

I suppose that the hired killers called their bosses to let them know that I was there before they carried out their orders. I am sure that Don Efra and Orlando Henao said, without a second thought, "Go right ahead." I was in charge of wielding the Cali Cartel's political power. It was two birds with one stone.

The men began shooting. Instinctively, I put my arms up, covering my head from the bullets. The force of the bullets threw me backwards, and I fell on a table that flipped over. This table served as my shield.

Once I was on the floor, I heard more gunshots. Oscar tried to get up and the man with the blue shoes shot him, again. Juan Carlos was shot in the aorta; he bled out immediately and his blood reached me, which led the killers to believe that I was dead. On the floor, all I could see was the movement of their feet; the one that moved the most, from one side to the other, was the one with the blue shoes. They fired ninety-five rounds. I got shot in the left wrist, in my right forearm, two times in my abdomen, once in the groin, and once in my knee. When I was falling, I got shot two more times, once in the back of my left leg, and the other grazing my right leg.

This fleeting moment felt like an eternity. Life passes us by in a second. I remembered the things that I had to repent for and, like a miracle, after having done that, I felt like I had connected with something that I will never be able to explain for sure: a moment of peace, tranquility, and relief that was interrupted by horrified screams.

"They killed him! They killed him!"

When I was on the sidewalk, the blood kept looking for a way out, and when I felt like I was about to collapse, as if sent by God himself, the two policemen showed up—a rare occurrence when a group has carried out an operation like this. A fundamental part of ensuring the mission's success is to make sure that the authorities do not show up while you are carrying it out. But I was not meant to die that day, and when I saw one of the policemen heading in my direction, my first reaction was to ask him to stand by me. When he called me "boss," I felt safe. Not because I was his boss, but because I felt his support, even though I still felt like I was about to die. For that reason, I said to him, "I'm going to die." The agent, with words that seemed to me the nicest words I had ever heard, said, "Don't you have someone to live for?" Again, I thought about my little daughter, about my wife, and what I wanted to do with my life if I survived. But the ambulance was still not there; the reporters were.

Near the restaurant, having been reporting on the death of the sports leader, Alex Gorayeb, there had been many reporters that headed straight toward the restaurant upon seeing so much commotion. They got there and recorded the images that would spread across the globe.

My guardian angel stayed with me until the ambulance got there, an event that revealed an even bigger problem, one worse than the attack itself.

Nicol's little brother, Fernando, had survived despite being shot in the head. Because we were not related, the policy made it clear that the first person that was to be taken to the hospital was the one who was in the worst condition. They wanted to only take Fernando and to leave me there. So, in a moment of extreme anger and frustration, I shouted at them, "Get the man in charge of this ambulance here, immediately!"

Despite my wounds and the loss of blood, when he got to me, I grabbed him by the neck and told him, "I can survive! Take me!"

For this reason, they put Fernando on the stretcher and let me sit on the side, where they usually take family members. The stretchers used on ambulances have these kinds of areas meant to be held onto; I grabbed onto one of them as if it was salvation itself, while still in the company of the policeman, who was trying to calm me down, telling me that there was nothing to worry about since we were almost at the hospital.

Later on, my wife told me that between the shooting, the death of my friends, the walk down the stairs, and the arrival at the hospital, only five minutes had gone by; to me it had been an eternity. Before passing out, I managed to ask forgiveness from the Christ of Buga for not having gone to see him that Friday. I felt bad; the night before I had made a promise and, now, my life was in his hands.

They carried me unconscious to the emergency room. A couple of weeks before this, I had been in that same room due to some parasites. During that visit, Doctor Alvaro Mejia had seen me. By the grace of God, Dr. Mejia, who knew my medical history, was there when they brought me in. Due to the loss of blood, Dr. Mejia put me under anesthesia immediately and began a race against time to save my life.

In the meantime, at the restaurant El Rodizio, the police were in charge of cleaning up the final results of the horrific incident. They recovered the bodies: ninety-five rounds had been shot with 9mm guns. Thirty-two of those hit Nicol Parra, ten ended the life of Oscar Echeverri, seven the life of Juan Carlos Delgado, and eight hit me.

As I struggled between life and death, my conscience traveled through valleys and mountains, passing through places that my father and uncle had, at one time, described to us as their respective places of birth, where they had gone on to endure childhoods filled with difficulties that would lead them to become what later on the whole world would know them as, the big bosses, the leaders of the Cali Cartel.

CHAPTER 2

My uncle was born in 1939 and my father in 1943. Their childhood was impacted by huge events in the history of Colombia, like the death of the great liberal leader Jorge Eliécer Gaitan, who set in motion a war between right- and left-wing ideologies which led way to a time period known as "La Violencia" (or "the Violence") in Colombia's history. The Violence which took place in Tolima and El Valle, was characterized by mass killings and forced displacement by bands of gunmen, today known as "paramilitaries." These gunmen worked for the wealthy politicians without being on an official payroll. These bands called themselves "Chulavitas" because of their origin in a subdivision north of Boyacá, and "Pajaros" if their origins were near El Valle.

The Pajaros, led by the legendary Leon Maria, alias "El Condor," and his right-hand man, El Chimbila, would threaten the wealthy, liberal landowners and force them to abandon their land. As a consequence of this activity, there was a massive displacement of rural populations into urban centers.

The Pajaros took advantage of the situation and, through legal shortcuts, bought the abandoned lands for a low price, and then, through back-door dealings with executives from the "Caja Agraria," obtained deeds that granted them ownership of massive chunks of land.

My father and my uncle were exposed to the effects of the displacement and the violence on multiple fronts. On one side, because of the abuse of my grandfather Carlos, and on the other, with what was happening around their communities.

In this environment, my uncle Gilberto, the oldest brother, was forced to abandon his studies, at the age of ten, in order to help my grandmother Rita look for ways to sustain their family.

He began selling flower vases at the local fairs in nearby towns. The entire family participated in this humble, entrepreneurial endeavor; some collected the empty bottles, others cut them, and my father—who has always been a brilliant artist—would decorate them. After they were finished, my uncle Gilberto would go out and sell them.

The daily act of providing for the family gave my uncle increased authority in the eyes of my grandma and his younger siblings. One particular day, being fed up with the violent abuse, he told my grandfather in brief but decisive terms that he was no longer welcome in their household. Carlos raised his hand in a menacing manner, but my grandmother stood up for my uncle, and together, they kicked him out of the house.

That moment would forever change the course of my uncle's life. From that day on, he took on the responsibility as head of the house. Psychologists call this "parentification," which is a sort of role reversal where the child is assigned the task of dealing with the needs of his family. This phenomenon often leads to significant neurosis that eventually manifests itself in other ways.

After moving to Cali, my uncle started a job at a pharmacy as a mail boy. Being out in the streets would eventually lead him to encounter a variety of illegal businesses that were becoming prominent all over the country, and for which my uncle held some kind of dark magnetism; between his job at the pharmacy, his participation in piracy, and his savings, he eventually opened up his own pharmacy.

Following his natural instinct as a businessman, in his tiny pharmacy, and with the knowledge accumulated from each town his family had moved through, he invented various healing syrups and potions for all kinds of ailments. Selling these medicines led my uncle to see just how lucrative the pharmacy business could be, and he would always remain involved in it. He also discovered that he could get his hands on many products not directly available to consumers and sell them among friends and at nightclubs. This mentality, fueled by his desire to provide his siblings with a proper education, would lead him to get involved in the illegal practice of stealing various medical supplies to later profit off of at his own pharmacy.

As a direct effect of the accord for peace between the liberals and the conservatives, and the founding of the "Frente Nacional," many of the Pajaros lost their jobs, and consequently, dedicated themselves to the only business they truly knew: delinquency. From theft, to kidnapping, and, in my uncle's case, to handling contraband. These gangs, or at least the surviving ones, would later evolve into the first mafias in Valle del Cauca, modeled after the corrupt organization of the "esmeralderos."

As the world's second producer of emeralds, Colombia exploited this resource. Aside from the legal exploitation taking place, there were certain areas known as "basureros de las minas," or the dumping site of the mines; these areas would become the central focus for continuous corruption, theft, and mafia. The activities that these groups took part in, ultimately controlled by the military, would bring to the region large sums of violence, death, and prostitution as a direct effect of the massive influx of cash.

It began becoming evident that, with the government fully behind these bands, the most dangerous crime in our country was corruption. The politicians bought control of the mines, without even pausing to think what this could do to the people of Colombia, who were just waking up from a nightmare of violence and death into what seemed to be a peaceful period where the only thing that mattered was to live, but to live well.

After these mafias began acquiring their own dynamic production and the United States called the country to attention, these same corrupt politicians tried to shut the organizations down, but it was too late. The business had grown out of their reach, out of their control. It was an easy economic alternative to a new emerging group in society with profound dreams and visions of ascending into a higher class.

As a logical consequence of the development of this new

business, the mafias modernized their methods. Some chose violence, others corruption, and, ultimately, they were able to infiltrate the political parties, the social strata, the armed estate, and even the revolutionary guerrillas. In the midst of the environment that engulfed the country and searching for a way to lift his family up from misery, my uncle, Gilberto, came across a man that would change his destiny: José "Chepe" Santacruz. This man, with his adventurous character, proposed the formation of a band of inland pirates to my uncle. In no time, they ransacked the entire southwest portion of Colombia, and their organization became known as "Los Chemas," named after the signature hairstyle—slicked back hair reminiscent of the Fifties—that they all sported.

Later, my uncle and "Chepe" would lay eyes on Benjamin Herrera for the first time. He was known in the criminal realm as "El Papa Negro" and was largely credited as the pioneer of narcotrafficking in the Valle del Cauca region of Colombia. He introduced this business to "Los Chemas," first with marijuana and soon after dealing cocaine.

"El Papa Negro" gave my uncle and "Chepe" the job of transporting the coca paste from Bolivia and Peru to Cali in order to process it so he could send the product to the drug market in the States.

As they acquired knowledge and experience, "Los Chemas" slowly began to take over the drug-trafficking business in Cali and started to dispatch their first shipments to North America.

Cocaine is derived from the coca leaf, which many indigenous tribes utilized as a gateway to attain a type of "spiritual" strength that they found themselves in need of as they faced the Spanish invaders; these conquistadors, aside from stealing their gold, wanted to enslave them and extinguish their way of life. Thanks to this miracle plant, they were able to survive the inhumane conditions of labor they were forced to endure.

My uncle Gilberto and "Chepe" decided to embark on their first trip with their first kilo, a large amount for that time. They journeyed across Central America: Panama, Costa Rica, Honduras, Mexico, and finally, the United States.

They arrived at the frontier with Texas, with their kilo of cocaine, ignoring the fact that this region was dominated by Pablo Acosta Villarreal—predecessor of Amado Carrillo Fuentes—a powerful cocaine and marijuana dealer whose center of operations was located in the Ojinaga frontier, in the state of Chihuahua.

If Acosta would have gotten wind that they were moving drugs through his region, my uncle and Chepe would have been better off facing the authorities. Luckily, they were able to get their merchandise across the border with little to no difficulty, and a month later, both men arrived in New York City, where they were shocked to see the high value of their product in this market. American society was hungry for drugs, and cocaine, of course, was supreme. In these days, a kilo of cocaine translated into $50,000 or even $60,000 in New York. In the narcos' world, nothing was as important as their first kilo.

After this trip and the successful sale of their first kilo, drug trafficking became my uncle's main activity, which he began perfecting by dividing up the workload: some would go to Peru and Bolivia to purchase the coca sulfate, others would transport it, and my father was in charge of converting the sulfate into chloralhydrate, the finished cocaine powder, in small laboratories in Valle del Cauca.

The coke was transported to the United States in various ways, and once there, others were in charge of distributing it at wholesale prices and others at retail until the product reached the discotheques, bars, and nightclubs in all major cities. In this way, the mafia satisfied the frustrations of a society that had just felt the effects of the war in Vietnam.

Through the division of responsibilities, one of the biggest drug-trafficking enterprises in the world began to develop. One which my uncle, and later my father, would project as a multinational similar to that of the whisky industry. Both activities were comprised of providers, standardized production, and excellent distribution channels. The difference is that one is legal and the other is not. From a moral viewpoint, I find little disparity between whisky and cocaine; alcohol consumption is the primary risk factor for death in America according to the World Health Organization.

With the power he was accumulating as a product of the large profits from his business, my uncle kept control over the lives of his siblings and created for them a life philosophy that through knowledge came progress. Thanks to this mentality, my father finished his secondary education in Santa Librada, one of the best schools in Cali, and went on to graduate from the University of Santiago de Cali with a law degree. My uncle had placed all of his hopes and expectations on his brother becoming a great lawyer, transforming into reality the unfulfilled dream he was forced to abandon as he took on the responsibility of looking out for the well-being of his younger siblings, a role that should have been my grandfather's.

His experience at university, the social changes of the time, and the bohemian lifestyle, shaped my father as a leading proponent of leftist ideas, but there was an event in his life that would deter him from his political idealism and would ground him in reality: he fell in love with my mother. Marrying my mother, without the blessing of my uncle, the patriarch of the family, led my father straight to misfortune. My uncle responded offensively: he threw my father out on the street and left him in poor shape economically. He stopped providing my father with financial support as he was furious because he believed that once married, my father would abandon his studies at the University of Santiago de Cali.

CHAPTER 3

The *boom* and the rebellious mindset of the Sixties shook Colombian society—one that was not equipped to handle a cultural shift of that magnitude—to its core. The youth was unable to find the spaces necessary to express and develop their dreams, and, influenced by the ideas of equality divulged by the socialist movement, found alternative ways to vocalize their nonconformity with society. Leftist guerrilla groups and pacifist movements that advocated for a cultural revolution in the arts and in the media emerged. Others, who were more daring, dared to change—or try to change—the social order, utilizing "easy money" obtained through the business of drug trafficking.

My uncle and father lived in a bohemian environment surrounded by intellectuals; through this ambience, they nourished the ideals they had inherited from my paternal grandfather, a liberal that lived in a time period dominated by conservatives. In the midst of this atmosphere of change, my father and uncle, along with many others, decided to challenge the bourgeoisie in hopes of fostering equality in society through whatever means necessary; this unleashed the birth of an emerging social caste.

The members of this new class which came from the countryside were not proletarians; they were rich, and their fortunes did not come from paychecks or family inheritance. Their wealth was the product of a business that was not legalized, and that, as such, was admired and accepted by those who benefitted from it; these newly rich citizens were able to fill spaces that the government, in its infinite short-sightedness, could not or did not want to see.

My parents were married under the Catholic Church, but, from the beginning, their marriage was destined to fail. Both had strong temperaments, and my father's affinity for drinking and the nightlife created a difficult climate, one in which a stable family life could hardly flourish.

After my uncle Gilberto threw him out, my father got a job working as a flight attendant for Avianca, but the demanding schedules the airline gave him put him at a crossroads: he could either leave his studies or his job. This was not an easy decision for him because he wanted to finish his degree, but my mother was pregnant with me and this was his main concern.

When I was born, in Cali on July 31, 1965, my father brought me to my uncle's house so that he could meet me. Surely, he took a liking to me, as he not only got over his anger, but also named himself my godfather. My uncle forgave my father and offered him a job working for him in the drugstore Monserrate which he owned. My father accepted this offer as his economic situation was continuously deteriorating. From that day on, my father and my uncle, once again, became inseparable.

My father rented a home by Circunvalar Avenue, where he, my mother, and I resided. In the beginning, I remember that we were happy, but not long after, under the influence of the friends he had made during his time attending university, my father was unable to abandon the bohemian lifestyle: he would leave one day and would return a week later.

Arguments were frequent occurrences in our home. I could not understand why there was always so much screaming. I witnessed many violent encounters between my parents, and would either find refuge hiding in a corner or would throw fits in a failed attempt to stop the horrible moments I was forced to live through.

My mother constantly questioned her decision to not listen to her father, who warned her numerous times to not get involved with a man like my father. My maternal grandfather, Manuel Antonio Abadia, an honest man, who forged for himself a small fortune in the transportation sector, greatly disliked the environment in which my father moved. He was always opposed to their relationship as he knew it was not beneficial for his daughter, but my mother's rebellious nature led her to ignore reason and end up with my father.

Before I turned five years old, it was discovered that my left kidney did not work properly; slowly, it was falling victim to atrophy, and it had to be taken out. The surgery was scheduled for August 2, 1970, two days after my birthday, which my parents celebrated like it was the last one I would ever have. The surgery took place in the Departmental Hospital of Cali by the gifted hands of surgeon Henry Garcia. After it was over, I remained in recovery for twenty-seven days, but Dr. Garcia managed to save my life. Ironically, I have some of the best memories with my parents from those traumatic days: it was the only time I had ever seen them work together, as a couple, to save the life of their only child. Unfortunately, too much pain and resentment existed in my mother's heart, while my father was completely submerged in the bohemian lifestyle.

The aggression continued, and my mother, fully knowing that my father could have a violent reaction to her actions, developed a plan to leave him, find another man, and take from him the one thing that perhaps he valued the most at that time: his son. Her vengeance knew no mercy: she was not interested in couples therapy or in simply filing for divorce stating "irreconcilable differences" as the cause. No, she decided to kidnap me so that she could punish my father in the worst way she could imagine. She made this decision in an effort to teach him a lesson, but I believe that I was the one most affected by it.

Without even knowing it, I helped her do it. I kept what she asked me to from my father. I never told him, which is why, in this moment, through my writing, I hope I can exorcise the pain that I have carried in my heart for many years—a pain that has, in a certain way, affected my character.

I remember that when we would go for ice cream, my father would say, "Something is up. What is happening?" Many times, he would pick me up and take me to my paternal grandmother's house and ask, "Where is your mother? Why have I not seen her lately?"

The truth was that many things were indeed happening, like,

for example, my mother was concocting a plan to leave Colombia with me. By forging his signature, she had managed to get a fake permit from a notary, which granted me permission to leave the country. And, in order to get me out of the country without raising any suspicion, she had traveled to Chicago three months prior to my departure. It was one of my aunts that took me all the way there with the fake authorization from my father.

The question that I would ask myself later was why I had lied to my father, having been such a small child and him so kind to me. I would come to find the answer in the loneliness I faced in the huge city that was Chicago … I did it for my mother, the person that brought me into the world. I witnessed her pain, and I felt solidarity toward her, so I lied to my father because I was loyal to my mother.

In my confused attempt to forget, I remember staring at the sunset in a beautiful city next to Lake Michigan. It was explained to me later that this body of water was a lake, for I thought, because of its enormity, that it was the ocean. The magnitude of the buildings and the grayish color of the city intrigued me. I wondered what my future would hold. I stared out of a wooden window—covered by multiple coats of paint, that was next to a steaming vent—at the way the snow fell; each snowflake that fell to the ground represented, to my desolate heart, every day I lost with my father.

I remember going into Kmart and running to the sections stocked with toys. I dreamed of owning everything I saw around me, trying to escape the reality of my situation. These were times of great scarcity for us. We survived on the little income that an undocumented person in this country could make, and my only toy was a little nuclear man that went with me everywhere.

The first relationship my mother had in Chicago was also marked with the stain of constant abuse. The situation that we lived through with my father was repeating itself. I felt frustrated, and my reaction was to lock everything up behind a wall of silence.

I went to a public school while my mother worked in factories.

I had few friends in school, virtually none. Thanks to my constant pleading, this abusive relationship was soon over. A new relationship began, and in this one I found the figure of a man who was not really paternal, but who offered me a friendship in which I found a sense of security. These were the only moments that brought me joy in the midst of my profound sadness because I had no father. I did not understand the reason that we were in this city, but she was my mother, and, like a good son, I thought my loyalty had to lie with her. In the end, the misery in which we found ourselves living was enough to make my mother rethink her decision, and she decided we needed to go back to Colombia.

After six years of absence, we returned to a place that was completely different. My father and uncle had risen to the status of businessmen. Their businesses had invaded a section of the economy reserved for an exclusive group of the bourgeoisie, one that would never forgive such an intrusion.

My uncle had founded El Banco de los Trabajadores and the corporate group Drogas la Rebaja, and he had acquired other drugstores. On top of this, he had purchased the radio station called Grupo Radial Colombiano and the Financiera Boyacá. Over time, Drogas la Rebaja would be administered by my aunt Amparo and her husband Alfonso Gil.

Six months after my return to Cali, in 1978, I took the initiative and called the headquarters of Drogas la Rebaja to schedule a meeting with my aunt Amparo. I had dedicated my first six months back in Colombia to learning how to read and write in Spanish. I had been spending the summer with my mother's family, who were from Yotoco, a small town close to Buga. There, in a massive house, many of my grandmother's sisters lived with my great-grandfather. I had enjoyed my stay there so much that I asked my mother to let me stay there for some time. She said yes and, during my time there, I established an excellent relationship with my great-grandfather, who told me stories that fascinated me. I have always enjoyed listening to my elders, and I have always gotten along better with those that are older than me. And it was in this town where they got me a tutor that helped me regain my knowledge of Spanish.

I meditated at length before I made the decision to call my father. I felt shame over the betrayal that I believed my mother and I had orchestrated. Even though my mother and my aunts had continually insisted, I did not do it until that day, when—after six months of vacationing in Yotoco—I woke up with every intention to confront the situation face to face, no matter the consequences.

The call was sort of funny. I asked to speak to my father and, after they told me he was not there, they asked who was calling. As soon as I said, "William Rodríguez, his son," there was a deadly silence on the other end of the line. My aunt Amparo's voice, the voice that asked me who I was one more time, broke the silence. We had a conversation, but what I remember from it the most is that she set down certain conditions that I had to follow in order to see my father.

I was asked to come to his office. That day, I was wearing a red shirt and some jeans. The minutes seemed eternal to me as I sat there waiting for him on a leather couch. When he finally appeared, I was flooded with conflicting emotions. The first, one that I was unable to control, was that of stubborn tears that streamed down my face. I will never forget that moment.

My father also found he did not know what to do. He had not seen me for six years, two of which he had spent searching for me all over the country. As a result of my disappearance and the abandonment from my mother, whom he was never able to forgive, he had become an alcoholic. I think men can forgive everything, except having our children taken from us.

He told me I had grown. I didn't need his words ... I needed a hug, but he kept talking and ordered me to follow him. We went across the street and into other offices that were part of La Drogueria, where we met with my uncle Gilberto, who, just like my father, looked at me over and over, up and down, with an expression of surprise.

I felt that something had changed within my father. He was not the man that I remembered. The man that did everything he could to please me, who let me climb on his lap so that I could steer his car, who was caring and kind. He was distant. Maybe he judged me because of what my mother had done to him, but I believe his behavior had more to do with the state of his family, which had severely changed. And, at the age of twelve, I was forced to start making difficult choices about my life.

My dad and my uncle gave me three options: I could live with my grandmother, with my uncle Gilberto and the new family he had established for himself in Bogotá, or with my cousins, my uncle's original family, that lived in Cali. I wanted to live with my father, but he had a new family and a new life. I immediately understood that I was not to abruptly enter his new home, but I also did not want to live with my mother since I blamed her for having separated me from my father.

I did not know his new wife, and my half-siblings were too little. It was not the same to live among children than to live with cousins that were my age. That was the justification that I used, but the truth is that I did not want to live under the same roof as the person that I wrongly blamed for coming between my mother and father.

It was evident that my uncle Gilberto led a double life. He had one family in Cali and another in Bogotá. His home base was Bogotá, where he had bigger business opportunities and greater access to power and to politics. My father lived in Cali, where the production took place. This is the reason that I decided to live with my aunt Mariela, my uncle's first wife, and my cousins. My aunt welcomed me into her home as if I was another one of her children, and my cousins treated me like a brother.

I had so much anger built up against my mother that I gave her the news that I was moving out like it was no big deal. "Why?!" she pleaded. I said nothing, while she went on and on about how they were turning me against her, an accusation that could not have been further from the truth. I alone had made the decision to move in with my cousins at my aunt Mariela's house.

At my aunt's house, I shared a room with my cousin Humberto, with whom I built a strong relationship; we bonded. Being the only child in a home can lead to a solitary life. When you are surrounded by siblings there are always activities, you share things, you coexist, you care about others: that was what living with my cousins was like. That was the beginning of my deep affection for that household.

The environment I found myself in was completely different to the one I had been in when I was in Chicago. I loved it, and at twelve years of age, I decided that was where I wanted to live for the rest of my life. Two factors drove my decision: the great affection I felt for my new-found family and the deep resentment I felt toward my mother, who I held responsible, to an extent, for everything I had gone through in Chicago.

I was incredibly happy in this new household. I found something I had never had before. And, even though I was not her son, my uncle's wife raised me with respect and rules: she taught me how to earn things in life. I was always a good student—not the best, but good—and she expected all of us to fulfill our duties as students. If I failed any class, they took away what I loved the most: soccer and going to the stadium.

During this time, I cared more about soccer than women. I had to do well, and, if at the end of the year, I failed any class, I would be banned from the family vacation. During high school, I failed only one class: drawing. In that house and with that family, I lived the best of my teenage years; life smiled upon us, and we felt lucky to have fathers that worked hard and maintained successful companies.

But that paradise would not last forever.

CHAPTER 4

After I decided where I wanted to live, and with whom, I had to decide what school I would be placed in. My father wanted me to attend the best schools. I applied to the Bennett School and to Pio XII. I purposefully failed the admission exams. I was always one of the only rebels in that patriarchy, and I showed them that, even though I never disrespected them, I was not afraid of them and, in the end, I always got my way. I wanted to study at the same school that my cousins were in: the school that belonged to Coomeva,

a cooperative where my aunt Mariela was a member.

In the beginning, when I first arrived from Chicago, my relationship with my father was distant and the only thing that united us was our passion for soccer. Just like he had built his own team, I created my own with the intention of emulating what he did. In the 9th grade, I built a tremendous team for our class. We were the champions of our school, beating even those in 10th and 11th grades, and, in the Coca-Cola tournament, we were crowned champions against twenty-seven teams.

My career as a soccer player and administrator was quickly dashed when I met Adriana, a brunette with caramel skin and a captivating figure, who introduced me to the world of passion and, soon after, to the drama that comes with sustaining a relationship that is suffocating and solely based on sex. This relationship would create many problems for me. One day, my aunt caught us and, in her prudent manner, gave me a choice: if I did not put an end to this relationship, I would have to speak to my father so that he could punish me or to speak to him about moving out of her house.

I tried to rebel, willing to face my father if necessary. But, soon after this, I found out Adriana was sleeping with another one of our peers from school. Being my first heartbreak, my first disillusion in love, I was faced with the consequences of my stubbornness, and, from this first great pain, I learned that this stubbornness only leads to blindness and blindness leads to resentment. In the end, this experience helped me refocus my energies toward following my dream to be a professional soccer player.

During this time, my cousins and I had no idea about the parallel business that our fathers were taking part in. We always saw them as prosperous businessmen, who worked hard so that we would never have to experience the difficulties that they had growing up. Their constant concerns were that we would succeed in school and that we would finish everything we started, which was why I knew that graduating from high school was a step in the right direction when it came to pleasing my father, but maybe he never noticed as he was out there chasing other things, like wealth and power.

After the death of minister Lara Bonilla, on April 30, 1984—which had been ordered by Pablo Escobar as a consequence for revealing the true nature of his business—we had a family meeting where they told us that my uncle Gilberto would be traveling outside of Colombia. He would be leaving for an undetermined amount of time—him and his second wife. The reason they told us: they wanted to rest.

At night, in our bedroom, my cousin Humberto and I discussed how weird this trip seemed to us. My uncle never stopped working; his vacations never lasted longer than a week, and him leaving like this, from one moment to the next, was strange. We went as far as to hypothesize that my uncle and his wife were facing marital problems and were going on a trip in order to fix them. It never occurred to us that this trip was a direct result of minister Lara Bonilla's death.

My uncle knew that with this insane act by Escobar, there would be an ensuing avalanche against anything that even hinted at drug trafficking, and that if an arrest warrant were to be issued by the United States, he would face the risk of being extradited.

Plus, he did not want to run the risk of having the world know who he really was in the underground world of drug trafficking.

My uncle flew to Panama, where he met up with his second wife, Gladys Miriam, and together they traveled to Madrid. At first, they attempted to maintain a low profile, but as the months went by and things began to cool down in Colombia, they began to lead a comfortable and lavish lifestyle. They bought property in the exclusive area known as La Moraleja, and would travel down the well-known streets of Madrid in luxury cars, frequently stopping at exclusive locations.

As fate would have it, Maria Elia, the wife of Jorge Luis Ochoa Vásquez, one of the leaders of the Medellín Cartel during the Eighties and Nineties, ran into Gladys Miriam in El Corte Inglés. This run-in led to my uncle and Jorge Luis developing a friendship and frequenting many luxurious places together, while spending large sums of money. Eventually, these extravagant expenditures caught the attention of the authorities, which corroborated the information sent from the United States regarding the true identity of these men that spent money without a second thought.

On November 20, 1984, my cousin Humberto and I found out that something had happened which we could not believe. The scandalous news that came from Europe was confusing to us. How was it possible that my uncle Gilberto was being accused of being one of the most powerful drug kingpins in the world? We had no idea that the United States demanded he be extradited, and even though the newspapers seemed to confirm it, we refused to accept this as the truth.

I spoke with my aunt Mariela, who initially denied that these rumors were true, but later, with a newspaper article in hand, I asked her again. She told me that it was a mistake, that her ex-husband had traveled to Madrid in order to invest in real estate, and they had mistaken this for something it wasn't. And, if I wanted to know any more, I had to ask my father directly.

I wondered why they had not told us anything about this; if

this was true, for those who knew about it, it would be easy, but for us, those who had constructed a social life filled with friends and decent people, it would be different—we would now be painted as criminals. It was not an easy thing to fall from heaven to hell from one day to the next.

We began analyzing the situation: on one side, we were educated people that had never participated in anything illegal, and who were, to the world, the children of respected businessmen from Cali; but, on the other side, there was the news that had come from Spain, the speculation surrounding my uncle Gilberto, and the many things we were being accused of. The situation impacted us deeply and we felt betrayed by our parents. Understanding this big mystery that had been concealed for years and that was just being revealed to us with blinding clarity led us all to the same place: if we had our families and business here, what were we to do? Where would we run to? Why should we? Having luxurious things was not a crime, and neither was being the children of Gilberto and Miguel Rodríguez Orejuela.

After giving it much thought, I arrived at the conclusion that I had to do what was expected of me: I needed to get into college and be the best, as a way to show my father that I supported him in these trying times. It was the one thing he had always demanded from us, and I was determined to do it. However, achieving this goal would be the beginning of a life of crucifixion for us; we would forever have to carry a cross on our backs, one that came as the result of a stigma that would fall upon us due to choices that had not been ours. In spite of this, I convinced my cousin that we had to confront the situation, and with our heads raised, we continued on.

My father wanted me to study economics, but due to everything that was happening to my uncle, I decided that my career should be law; maybe, in this way, I wanted to follow in my father's footsteps in order to surpass him. I took the entrance exam and interviewed at the university like everyone else, thinking this would be the best way to go about it. I believed that becoming a lawyer could one day help my family out in the battle that had just begun.

My uncle had been captured on November 15, 1984, as he was exiting his house on the street General Oraa in Madrid. The United States had sent a request to the Spanish government, which led the operation to fall under the jurisdiction of Interpol.

While my uncle was kept in the shadows, my father was left in charge of all their businesses—legal and illegal. One of the first decisions he made was to close a series of businesses that had little to no growth and were unprofitable. He chose to focus on the ones that were solvent and had a bigger participation in the market, like the pharmacies, the pharmaceutical laboratories, radio stations, and, among others, his beloved soccer team: América de Cali, his greatest passion. It was during this time that he established a business relationship with Hélmer "Pacho" Herrera, the biggest distributor of cocaine in New York, which allowed the cartel's distribution channels to grow exponentially.

My father, the obsessive, meticulous, disciplined man that he is, set saving his brother from the fate that awaited for him in the United States as his most pressing priority. To do this, he brought together the best judicial team in the country. He wanted to put up a fight, while still maintaining and growing the Rodríguez family's empire.

Having been younger than my uncle, he had learned from him how to stay ahead in the biggest businesses, an innate quality that my uncle had applied in their most successful businesses. For example, my uncle had made sure that 70% of Drogas la Rebaja belonged to him, leaving 30% for my father.

The man that would spearhead the judicial team built by my father was Alvaro Holguin, a man that had been close to my father since their days as classmates in the school Santa Librada de Cali. Holguin's older brother, Armando Holguin, a man that had been my father's professor in school and had been a senator of the republic, was also on the team.

The Holguin brothers were in charge of working, alongside the attorneys they had in Spain, to get my uncle's extradition to be to Colombia, instead of to the United States. For this reason, they had to get the Colombian government to press charges against him for drug trafficking, so that he could be requested to return to Colombia to face the judicial system. In Spain, the team of attorneys was led by Joaquin Ruiz and Carlos Cuenca, the latter serving more as a dependable lobbyist.

My uncle spent thirty-five months in two correctional centers in Spain: one in Meco, which was in Madrid, and one in the port of Santa Maria. During this time, I had a serious conversation with my father, who gave me a base explanation about what was happening. He intended to continue on with the businesses. He confessed that they had conducted some illegal businesses in the past, but he assured me that it was not like that anymore; and, in this way, he convinced me that what was happening to my uncle was unfair.

Since I was in the first semester of my studies to become an attorney, what my father told me motivated me to fly to Spain and offer my uncle words of comfort and support. It was the right thing to do: this injustice that (I believed) he was experiencing had to be exorcised in some way, even if it was just within the family.

Before I went to visit him in prison, I suffered an accident in my uncle's residence in la Moraleja as I headed to have lunch with my cousins Claudia Pilar and Juan Carlos. When I reached the condominium's iron gate, it for some reason became deactivated. In an effort to activate it again, I introduced my left arm—I am a lefty—between the bars so that I could reach the button that would turn them on. I did not calculate my movements correctly and became trapped between the bars and the stone wall. The door was lodged between my shoulder and neck, and it began to choke me slowly; I could hear the chains rattling and had no way to stop it.

I couldn't breathe and felt like my head was going to explode. I thought I was going to die; I lost consciousness for a brief moment. I felt like I was floating, and with no explanation, one of the springs broke, and I was strangely thrown out from the grips of the door and fell to the floor with no strength to hold me. The pressure had ruptured some blood vessels in my face. When I returned to Cali and after I assured them that I was no longer in danger, my family joked that I had been so bored with my life in Spain that I had tried to get an iron gate to strangulate me.

This had been an extremely painful and traumatic experience. The amount of time that my brain stopped receiving oxygen could have caused irreversible damage to my brain. Luckily, this was not the case, and for this reason, I consider this incident as my second close encounter with death. The first had been at five years of age, when I had to get my kidney taken out, in one of the first surgeries of this kind in Cali.

When I visited my uncle in prison, after the accident, he was left extremely concerned from seeing my disfigured face and my bloodshot eyes, and immediately reached out to my father. Together, they decided to send me to Miami so that I could have all kinds of medical exams done.

As these events were taking place, the working relationship between my father and Hélmer "Pacho" Herrera had started producing results. They had, virtually, the entire market in New York under their control. Pacho orchestrated an extraordinary system of distribution, and my father a perfect production: this international exporter of cocaine was growing and it was evident. During this boom, my father traveled to Bogotá from Monday to Friday, and stayed in the presidential suite at the Hotel Tequendama. In this suite, he held all kinds of meetings with politicians, judges, district attorneys, and businessmen. He also made time to meet with celebrities for social calls.

Rivers of money circulated in Colombia, buying consciences— particularly those of the aristocracy that had direct influence over judges. My father took advantage of the strong anti-American feeling that existed in Spain. After an arduous effort, alongside his attorneys, my father was able to get a favorable verdict from

Spain's Supreme Court, which was presided over by the illustrious Antonio Hernández Gil.

On June 27, 1986, my uncle arrived at the Villahermosa prison in Cali. Before he was processed into this prison, my father had been able to arrange to be taken to a house so that we could all see him and spend a few moments among family. These were emotional moments for all of us. My uncle was calm: having been saved from an extradition to the United States was something that needed to be celebrated, at least for twenty-four hours. We said our tearful goodbyes, while he expressed sincere optimism. It was ideal to have his temporary office in Cali, where he was surrounded by family, and where he could resume all of his usual activities.

On Saturdays, we had to wake up early to go visit him. We had to make a long line before getting in. Inside of the prison, we realized that the murals that had been created by various artists had been turned into waiting areas for their corporation by my father and uncle. After dealing with all of his guests, my uncle dedicated an hour to his family. Ironically, we were never guests there; instead, it was more of an obligation imposed by my father, who, in his fantasy world, believed that it was important for my uncle to be visited by family.

Regarding his presence in this prison, the most popular topic of conversation among the inmates was that Mr. Rodríguez was among them—the leader of the Cali Cartel, one of the owners of the soccer team América de Cali, a team that had reached notorious levels of national and international recognition after having won four consecutive national championships.

The inmates were hopeful, as they expected that the conditions in which they lived in were about to change. Many knew that they would become part of the Rodríguezs' roster, in the same way that they knew that with the reunion of these brothers would come even more growth for their empire. A reality from which we were not exempt seeing as our allowances increased. Our security team also changed, going from basically non-existent to two bodyguards per family member.

While we were being introduced, via our studies, to governing theories that ranged from Marxism to extremely conservative ideals developed by American presidents, those same Americans would not give up their initiative to extradite my uncle to the United States. The legal charges over drug trafficking that had been started in Colombia, the same ones that had existed in Spain, continued their steady progression, a fact that would test the limits of our power.

Simultaneously, at my father's request, the organization worked on influencing the political and judicial processes in order to make the possibility of extradition disappear, a notion that was headed toward President Belisario Betancur's desk from the Ministry of Justice. To ensure a desirable result for my father and uncle, they had to arrange for a meeting of the Council of Ministers so that the people they had on the inside could stop the process.

They managed to stop President Betancur from signing the order of extradition. The score stood at Rodríguez Brothers: 2, United States: 0. Once again, my father had saved my uncle, demonstrating that the methods he used were more effective than terrorism and violence, mechanisms utilized by Pablo Escobar.

My uncle began attending audiences and they began to develop a strategy so that he could return to freedom; finally, he was convicted for drug trafficking by the honorable judge Tobias Ivan Poso. After completing his sentence, my uncle tried to retake complete control over the businesses, but he would encounter a new reality: the power and all of the connections—political, judicial, and within the drug-trafficking world—were in the hands of someone else: those of my father, Miguel Rodríguez Orejuela.

I was never witness to a single argument between them over this change of leadership, and no comment was ever made about it. The only things that were overwhelmingly clear were that my father was now number one, that he intended to continue leading every aspect of the organization, and that he was not considering turning any power over to my uncle Gilberto. My father recommended that his brother focus on the development of the legal businesses—like the chain of pharmacies Drogas la Rebaja, and the Kresffor laboratories—on getting his freedom back, and, most of all, on spending time with the family.

In spite of these changes in leadership, my father and uncle always had, and continued on maintaining through the years, a tight, enigmatic relationship that surpasses any other relationship of loyalty and respect that I have ever known. My father saw my uncle Gilberto like a father, his natural leader, the one person he admired above anyone, his teacher. On my uncle's side, he felt an eternal gratitude toward his brother for saving him from extradition to the United States by achieving the Machiavellian scheme of extraditing him to Colombia instead, and for having grown his business and his economic empire, which had made them even more rich and powerful.

It is evident that these ties were built from the familial bond, and, in their own way, they tried to instill this in us. Their affinity for one another was a result of specific conditions of their time that had been fundamentally marked by intense suffering and poverty; this affinity became even more evident when they were finally reunited. As a strategy and for their own personal satisfaction, my father and uncle used their power and influence to occupy spaces that naturally should only lie with the State, as they tried to make Cali a sort of haven, a city where people lived in harmony.

They established a set of rules for the criminal world, and any group or individual that dared break these rules of coexistence would pay. When any rule was broken, they analyzed the facts and, afterwards, the culprits were summoned and called to order. If they continued on defying their rules and disrespecting them, they were taken care of. Paradoxically, today there are many citizens of Cali that miss this set of rules and expectations that were established by the Cali Cartel, due to the severe insecurity that now plagues my beloved city.

While my uncle carried out his sentence, I continued my studies and the entire family continued to enjoy the fruits that resulted from the prosperity of the empire. Cali and her citizens lived through an era filled by tranquility and peace, but, soon after, winds that spoke of conflict and tension began to blow into the city from other places of the country, due especially to the incremental progression of the war waged by Escobar on the State.

My uncle was released from Cali's Villahermosa prison in October of 1987. It was another day filled with celebration. He was happy to be surrounded by family; joy filled the atmosphere. One specific event from the evening caught my attention: a man that we had never seen before showed up to the gathering. He was welcomed by and waited on directly by my father and uncle with a large amount of deference. My cousins and I exchanged looks of confusion: we were surprised by this special treatment, which was usually only reserved for Chepe. This was the official presentation of the fourth musketeer, Mr. Hélmer "Pacho" Herrera. Invaluable to the organization, he was in charge of receiving and distributing all of the product that was exported to New York. We were not the only ones surprised: my uncle did not know him and his presence in our home had a purpose.

After winning the battle against the gringos and the judicial system of Colombia, my father and uncle still tasted victory on their tongues, but they had a new worry. After having achieved financial stability, it was not in their best interests to continue to defy the United States. Their triumphs had only been simple battles, and my father and uncle knew that, in the end, they would end up losing the war. It was the perfect moment to retire, adopt a new way of life, and legitimize their fortunes.

This gathering with their partners was not just to update each other on the state of their business, it also held a sort of reflective character that was aimed at reaching a mutually beneficial consensus in favor of the idea of retiring from the illegal business in order to focus on their legal empire. This was the best decision they could have taken, not only for them, but for the family, too.

But, in life, when you do not make decisions, they are made for you. And, in the end, this momentary contemplation was overshadowed by the certainty of war that came as news arrived that would put them between the sword and the wall, and which would take them to the point of no return, from which not even the family itself would survive.

CHAPTER 5

Our family was living in peaceful times. We had gone through a period of much stress and worry due to the legal process against my uncle in Spain. My father had been able to steal my uncle from the hands of the gringos and to return him to freedom; a feat many had considered impossible. We saw a return to those prosperous times in the Eighties when we had been a family that enjoyed peace and prosperity. But this had simply been an illusion that lasted briefly due to the fact that my uncle and father had been brought out of the shadows and were now well-known characters from the world of drug trafficking, and with the influence they had won through their triumph, they stepped the toes of many that would never forgive them.

After that whole ordeal, my father Miguel and my uncle Gilberto were seriously considering retiring from the criminal scene. They had amassed a large fortune. Their business affairs were on solid ground and their children had started to take over the management of their industrial empire; they saw this as the perfect moment to legitimize their businesses and to return to living a life under the radar. But an unexpected situation would push them toward the point of no return.

In 1987, Pablo Escobar was in the middle of an insane war against the Colombian State. In order to continually carry out his terrorism, he constantly requested the economic and military aid of the other organizations that dealt in the drug-trafficking trade. Many complied out of fear: if they refused him, they would be annihilated by his military organization. The Cali Cartel, led by my father and uncle, never aided him; because of their ideology, their war against the State was always carried out judicially, and, even though they tried to negotiate with Escobar in other ways, as they thought about retirement, they knew that sooner or later he would seek to punish them for their defiance.

An incident that occurred in the United States due to the theft of some drugs would mark the beginning of a conflict that would change our lives forever: the war that Pablo Escobar declared against us. Faced with this new reality, my father and uncle abandoned their efforts to legitimize their business and continued to participate in the lucrative business of drug trafficking; if they were to confront the murderous organization from Medellín led by Pablo Escobar, they needed large sums of money.

Unaware of what was going on around me, I continued on with my routine. During the week, I studied, and on the weekends, I played soccer, went to our country house, or stayed in Cali with my friends; I tried to spend the rest of my time with my family. I was about to finish my fifth semester, and if we were in any danger, we never knew it, until we started to notice drastic changes in our security detail: they reinforced our bodyguards; we went from two bodyguards to five; they changed from revolvers to 9mm guns, machine guns, and shotguns; our house was reinforced with more personnel; my father and uncle went from having four men in their detail to a minimum of twelve; we also began to notice weapons in our security detail that were only supposed to be used by the national army, like long-distance rifles.

One of those days, during a break between classes, I was chatting with a classmate in the hall on the first floor of the building. At some point, I noticed a beautiful woman in the distance that was coming from playing a game of basketball. She was walking straight toward where I was, a fact that surprised me. I will never forget what I felt when I saw her gorgeous brown eyes and her beautiful figure. She said hi to my friend and kept going, giving me a sideways glance that awakened my curiosity over who this beautiful woman was.

She was a student in economics, my friend informed me, and said that, if I wanted, he would introduce me to her immediately. There was nothing I would have wanted more than to meet her right then and there, but I had learned to rein in my emotions, so I told him that everything happens at the right time.

Due to the changes in our security detail, my cousin Humberto and I discussed that something strange was happening. Something grave surrounded our family and, although we were taught not to ask, I did not want to keep on wondering, so I decided to pay my father a visit. It's worth noting that I needed to schedule an appointment with anticipation in order to see him.

As fate would have it, I ran into my old schoolmate, Nicol. It was a pleasant surprise. We reminisced about old times and, after a hurried recounting of our adolescence, I wondered what he was doing at my father's house. For a brief moment, I thought they might have some business together, but Nicol, as if he had read my mind, said, "I work for your father."

His answer did not satiate my doubt. He realized this fact and, lowering his voice, told me that he was working in a special group in my father's security detail. This select group was led by a man nicknamed "El Pecoso." This man had been in the cartel's ranks for many years, and he had helped my uncle in a war that he had won against a band of kidnappers in Bogotá in the late Seventies.

I thought that my old friend was just the person that I needed in order to update myself on the recent changes that were going on around me. Through him, I discovered that we were in an all-out war against the Medellín Cartel. A chill went through my entire body; I felt fear—for my life and the lives of my family members.

Even though my father and uncle were in a dangerous business, we had never felt the effects of it. They had made sure that this was so, since one of their objectives was to keep the family out of that world entirely. Doing this would have negated all their efforts. If they had risked their lives to amass a fortune for the family, it wouldn't have made sense to put said family in danger. A fact that had meant security and tranquility for all of us.

But when Nicol told me of the various actions planned by Escobar against my father and uncle, I began to worry. That day,

I found out about various assassination attempts that had been thwarted due to the intervention of this select group of men, who risked their lives on the street to protect them from the killers sent to Cali by Escobar. I became even more concerned when he told me what to me was not only a revelation, but a confirmation of total chaos: that the assassination attempt that took place in the Monaco building in Medellín, which was the permanent residence of Escobar and his family, had been organized by the Cali Cartel.

Then I understood why my father and my uncle had decided to send us to Miami. I had questioned this decision, but I received an irrefutable answer: "It's an order!" My opposition stemmed from two reasons: one was that I did not want to miss my classes at the university, and the second was the woman I had met, the basketball player. More than wanting the end of this insane war against the Medellín Cartel, I wanted to meet this woman.

Our life in Miami was fun at first: we found ourselves in a city that was created for tourism. But as days, and then months, went on, I began yearning for home and for my day-to-day life. I spoke with the big bosses. I told them that exile was not the solution to anything, that we were in danger no matter where we went in the world. It was not easy for any of us to have to abandon the life we had in our household from one day to the next. Our existence had been reduced to living inside of a bubble, and we needed to go back to reality.

In the midst of the war, we returned to Cali. When we arrived, my father and my uncle got us together to warn us that even though we could all go back to our routines, we had to promise that we would lead disciplined lives and that we would follow the rules imposed by our security; whoever refused to comply would be taken out of the country immediately.

It was in those circumstances that I met Maria Garcia. My friend, whom I had driven insane with incessant questioning, introduced me to her on one of those days. She knew who I was due to all the rumors that were circulating in school, so she simply said hello in a cordial manner, said goodbye, and walked away. As I watched her leave, I thought about the thing that had caught my attention the most about her: her beautiful smile had put me under a spell. They say that opposites attract, and she was my complete opposite. Happy and kind. That day, even though she showed no interest in me, she captivated me, and something in me thought that she would be the love of my life.

Being a member of the Rodríguez Orejuela family was, in itself, something that drew admiration from some but rejection from others. It's only logical: if you are the son of one of the most notorious drug traffickers, people think that you must also be in the business of trafficking drugs. Maria was not exempt from thinking this way. It was an uncomfortable situation, and, if I handled it incorrectly, I could kiss any chance of having a serious relationship with her goodbye.

I searched for her on campus and found her, buried in books. Getting the relationship started was not easy. I was known for being a player, a fact that led to her rejection. Nonetheless, I persisted. I wanted this woman for me, and I became her shadow: no matter where she was, I would try to find an excuse to be there as well. This was unlike my usual manner of being, as I was used to easy conquests, but she was different. I discovered that when something is not easy to attain, the satisfaction at the end is even greater.

One insignificant coincidence helped me get closer to her heart: we discovered that we had met before. Maria was that girl that lived one block away from my maternal grandmother's house, next to Estación Avenue, so that day, in between nervous laughter, we concluded that our paths had already crossed once.

*****

For the first time in Colombia's history, a criminal had gotten the aristocracy from Bogotá—which had held the strings of power in their hands for over fifty years—on their knees. As a result of the horrifying actions taken by Escobar, the oligarchy felt vulnerable. In actuality, there were few figures in the government that had been brave enough to stand up to Escobar. Today, those few, paradoxically, are being persecuted by the justice system due to fictitious tales created by criminals that were part of the Medellín Cartel. Among those that were persecuted are Gustavo de Greiff, who was the first to lead La Fiscalía General de la Nación between 1992 and 1994; General Miguel Maza Márquez, director of the Administrative Department of Security (DAS) between 1985 and 1991; and General Octavio Vargas Silva, who was the director of the National Police during the era when Pablo Escobar fell.

After the murder of Luis Carlos Galán, something happened that would transcendentally alter the war against the Medellín Cartel. Many leaders of the nation, in an attempt to preserve their own interests, asked another criminal organization, the Cali Cartel, to join forces with them to defeat Pablo Escobar. Although many will deny it, there did exist a pact between criminals and the bourgeoisie.

The military body of the government and the "señores de Cali" joined forces to liberate Colombia of that agent of evil that had terrorized the country in the Eighties and early Nineties. I am not the only one that has said so, my uncle said it too during a radical interview, and it is written in many books that have been written on the subject.

After the horrifying murder of Galán, our security detail became a constant worry. I was barely able to see Maria, a factor that made our budding relationship even more difficult. My friend Nicol kept me updated on the monstrous acts carried out by each band. In six months, my father had miraculously escaped two attempts on his life with explosives; thanks to the opportune intervention by that special group led by "El Pecoso," they had been able to find the assassins sent to murder us from Medellín.

I found out about a plan that I find to be absolutely insane when I look back at it today, but that, in that moment of war, I saw as a way to save the country, my family, and my relationship with

Maria. They hired four mercenaries from England to carry out an assassination plan against Escobar at la Hacienda Nápoles, his recreational country home. In preparation, they had managed to infiltrate a person that would provide us with the details regarding a party that was being prepared to celebrate the qualification of Medellín's soccer team, El Nacional, to the finals of the Copa Libertadores.

Nicol was part of the group of men that would arrive by land to supplement the efforts of the Englishmen, who were planning to bomb the home from two helicopters. In that moment, Nicol asked me for a favor: if he was killed, I had to swear to him that I would give the money that he would be paid to his wife. I meditated on this for a moment. This would mean getting involved in matters that I was not supposed to know about, but Nicol was my friend, so I promised him that I would do as he asked.

Everything was ready. People believed that this would be the final move of this hellish war. Everything had been agreed to and planned in the airways. It was a complicated maneuver due to the difficult access to the mountainous area that surrounded the home. The intricacy with which the act had been planned gave those that were executing it some confidence. The only thing that they could not account for was the irresponsibility of one of the pilots, who had gone out the night before and gotten drunk in an effort to quell his nerves, and on the day of the operation, he had crashed his helicopter against the last peak in the mountains.

The news regarding the failure of this mission was transmitted quickly back to Cali and it generated even more confusion and worry within the cartel. Having been sure that this plan would work, my father and uncle had told us to continue on with our normal lives, for they had a surprise for us. But they were the ones who would end up being surprised when they realized that once again luck had favored Escobar.

One night I was awakened by a loud explosion. I grabbed the radio that we used to communicate internally, turned it on, and through it heard, "Alfa one entering Ciudad Jardín." Ciudad

Jardín was the vicinity where we lived; "alfa one" was the code used to refer to my father. Instinctively, I dropped the radio, put on some clothes, and ran outside.

In the parking lot, one of the guards, upon seeing the angst across my face, asked me, "What's wrong, sir?" I couldn't hear anything. I could only think of my father. I turned the car on and, realizing I had no bodyguards with me, told the guard to come with me; the poor man had no idea what to do. I barely gave him a chance to think.

I arrived at the street where the explosion had taken place and, looking at the remains of three houses that were located at the beginning of the street, I felt panicked. I started to search for the vehicles that carried my father around. I could not see them, so I imagined the worst. I tried to get my feelings in check. What was happening was maddening; I thought about what the Escobar family would have felt if the attempt on Escobar's life at the Monaco building had been successful. Suddenly, "El Pecoso" arrived.

"Sir, don't worry. Your father is OK," he said.

I felt like my soul had returned to my body. "Where is he?!" I asked.

"At House 1," he answered. "But we have to leave. It is not safe for you to be here." And he led me to his car which was guarded by other men.

As I looked at the horrific scene through the car's window, I remembered the guard I had taken with me and thanked him for his companionship.

The next morning, I received a call from Maria. She wanted to know what had happened, since she had heard about the assassination attempt on the news. I took advantage of the situation and asked her to lunch. She said yes. Moments later, I received a report from our security detail that recounted the events of the previous night to me. Two men and one woman, hired by Escobar, had bought a house two months prior in Ciudad Jardín. During this time, they had gathered intelligence regarding my father's movements. They had calculated that he would be passing through that street at around eleven or twelve at night. They installed a car filled with 100 kilos of dynamite at a strategic point so that they could detonate it as he passed by. Miraculously, my father had decided to return home earlier that night. When the hired killers realized that their plan had failed, they tried to return the car to the garage but had such bad luck that a neighbor had been using his remote control to turn on his TV and it set the dynamite off by accident. My father's guardian angel had saved him from death.

Escobar's war against the current order had managed to reach such an extreme that he had no problem offering up a sum of money for every cop that was killed depending on their rank. It was the most difficult time for policemen in Medellín: Escobar offered 2 million pesos for each normal cop, 5 million for each noncommissioned officer, and 10 million for each officer.

Due to this violent initiative that had severely increased the rate of mortality for cops, the Search Unit of the National Police was established. This was a special command made up of elite guerrilla fighters that had been trained in the United States. Most of them had attended courses at the main international intelligence agencies and were, over everything else, men of infallible integrity that could not be bought.

Such insanity was only met with more insanity. My father and uncle did not skimp out on a single dollar that could be put to finally achieving what they believed would be their greatest victory, maybe with the hope that they would be absolved in society's eyes, and would receive gratitude for ridding Colombia of this horrible man.

What we overlooked was that in order to help maintain this special command, my father and uncle had to contribute a weekly sum of about 150,000–200,000 dollars a week. Not only this, but they had also offered a reward for every man that worked for Escobar, not just his security team, but also those that executed his terrorist acts and were recognized by the State's security organizations, and were under the command of men like aliases Popeye, Pinina, Tyson, La Kika, Tomate, El Chopo El Arete, El Mugre, and many more criminals that worked with them.

Once the formation of this Search Bloc was agreed upon, my father's friends suggested that it should be spearheaded by someone that had ties to our region, El Valle del Cauca. Someone that was respected by the institutions and was someone within their means. As was recommended, they named Colonel Danilo González as commander of this group. He achieved many impressive results against Escobar's military structure and logistics team, but he was removed from power just a few months after having assumed his role because of pressure placed on the State by highly influential men in government that protected Escobar. My father and uncle's allies responded by pressuring the State to put Danilo González back in command. Their pressure, mixed with the lack of activity that had befallen the Search Bloc, got González his position back, and he immediately began working on getting Escobar.

Escobar was able to evade the traps set for him by the Search Bloc, and, even though they could hear his voice, they were unable to capture him. His ability to move around Medellín and her surroundings was such that he was able to continue carrying out his terrorist deeds and pulling the strings of power. He has been, I stress one more time, the only Colombian from humble beginnings that was able to bring the oligarchy to its knees; they were forced to comply under the force of his heinous acts and to pass the generous legislature that served as a foundation for his surrender.

On June 19, 1991, the Colombian citizenry and the entire world became witnesses to Escobar turning himself in and to his imprisonment inside of the famous prison known as La Catedral, a new private mansion, something that would eternally shame our government. His surrender had been achieved through the supposed collaboration of the senile priest Rafael García Herreros, founder of the extraordinary Minuto de Dios initiative, who negotiated the terms of a dignified imprisonment and care with the National Army inside of a jail that had been constructed by Escobar himself.

The fact that Escobar was in prison did not stop him from continuing to carry out his terrorist acts, but it did add a complication to the efforts made by the Rodríguez Orejuela brothers. Congressmen, magistrates, businessmen, and politicians of all kinds begged them for a meeting so that they could be protected from the violence that they could easily fall victim to. With Escobar in jail, the government could evade any blame for anything that occurred. If a criminal was in prison, then technically he should be unable to continue carrying out illegal acts, but Escobar demonstrated that the steps taken legally were simply a way to look good on paper, but the illegal ones were the ones that could resolve or worsen any issue.

Since, in one way or another, their location was known, those that wanted to see Escobar meet his end could not lower their guards even if he was imprisoned and his imprisonment benefitted the Cali Cartel. During this time, this cartel expanded its routes and its business with the international mafias and continued to grow: everyone preferred working with men who inspired confidence, like the Rodríguez Orejuela, and not with men like Escobar who were unpredictable and, frankly, not well.

When I discovered that the new plan hatched by the Cali Cartel was to bomb La Catedral, I really felt like there was no way back in this war. It was difficult not to want his demise. The report that claimed that he had cut up his partners' bodies and had disposed of them through the bathrooms of the prison was repulsive to me; I could not condone that way of acting.

In order to carry out this plan, my father and uncle hired Jorge Salcedo Cabrera, the son of a well-known general, sort of a local mercenary that sold his hands to the highest bidder. I ran into him multiple times at my father's home. He was, or maybe still is, one of those people that inspire a profound distrust at first sight. I never liked that man. His eyes seemed insincere to me. They say that the eyes are the windows to the soul, and this man always gave me a bad feeling in my gut.

My father ordered Jorge Salcedo to fly to Costa Rica and buy four bombs, known in the black market as "papaya bombs" and cost approximately 6 million dollars. In this country in Central America, Salcedo was able to negotiate the deal. According to their plan, they would first send two of the bombs—these made it to Colombia—and then they would send the other two. The second two never made it back to Colombia as they were supposedly discovered by authorities when he was trying to send them, and he, miraculously, evaded arrest. Salcedo went back to Colombia and informed my dad and uncle what had occurred. It has always remained a mystery how this man managed to evade arrest.

The bombs that made it back could not be detonated from any plane. To do this, they needed to use a plane with characteristics similar to those of MiG planes, that were engineered by the Soviets, which put a stop to the plan, and, once again, left everyone feeling frustrated. My father and uncle kept all of this from us, but I would end up finding out through Nicol.

Generally, I would always dine with family such as my aunt and my cousins, and our conversations would continually end up, sometimes unintentionally, covering the topic of the situation that we imagined we were living in. All we had to do was watch the news to learn of the state of terror that the country was in, and we were no exception. Through my relationship with Nicol, I was the one that had the most information about the events that were taking place in the war against Medellín. I was always quite prudent and only shared what I knew with my older cousins; we argued about the topic, we thought about it extensively, imagined possible scenarios, and we ultimately ended up asking ourselves the same question: Why did my father and uncle keep this from us? It was like they were trying to shut our eyes to a reality that was inescapable. We told ourselves that they did it to protect us, to keep us from getting involved; and, sometimes, we even questioned whether they cared about us at all. I believe that they made this choice because, strategically, if you are in an all-out war, it is better to keep your family at a safe distance. This way of thinking is based on what I now believe is an illogical belief: that a narco always puts his family first as a justification for what he does. But, in the end, it's always the family that ends up losing because we were placed in a state of limbo, where we could not be one thing or the other, and that was my biggest argument with them. I wanted to be normal, to lead a normal life, to go out with my friends, to go to school, to work, to enjoy my life, but I was unable to do so due to the constant state of war that we lived in, and even when I was allowed to do anything, I was placed under strict limits.

As military experts suggest, a war is one if one can anticipate when it is going to end, but Escobar was never able to see this, and the other drug traffickers, who he forced to comply with his war, grew wary. The group known as "Los Doce del Patíbulo" decided to fly to Cali and ask my father and uncle for protection from Pablo. This was how the PEPES were born, an acronym that stood for People Persecuted by Pablo Escobar. These men knew his organization from the inside and, with the information they provided, a plan was made to kill any person that stood with Escobar, including his lawyers and family, which would help debilitate him.

During this time, the United States aided the Search Bloc with a group from Delta Force and several CIA agents dispatched to Colombia. These men knew that the Cali Cartel provided substantial aid to the Bloc, but they never said anything as they believed that the end justified the means.

Pablo Escobar ran away from La Catedral. His men in command were murdered or simply captured. It was just a matter of time. My father and uncle had offered 10 million dollars as a reward for his death, which made it known to everyone that his capture would be more of a hit than anything else.

Thanks to the Search Bloc's tactics and Escobar's growing

need to know something about his family's whereabouts, they were able to triangulate a call that he made to his son. Escobar was found and, later, murdered alongside "El Limon," his last standing accomplice.

The day after this event, which had brought happiness to the entire country but infinite sadness to his family, the leaders of the Search Bloc went to Cali, in order to collect the 10-million-dollar reward that my father and uncle had offered for the murder of Pablo Escobar Gaviria.

Modern history's ultimate judgment must recognize and acknowledge the part played by the Cali Cartel, led by Miguel and Gilberto Rodríguez, as the main actors in the war against Pablo Escobar that put an end to six years of war, uncertainty, and fear, not only for the entire country, but for the Rodríguez family.

Days after his death, due to some accusations made by his son in anger and pain, my father and uncle welcomed Escobar's widow and son. In this meeting, they promised them two things: that the war was over and they were to be protected. Nothing would happen to Escobar's family. They even suggested that his family leave the country; Escobar had accumulated many enemies, and no one would be able to contain them all.

*****

That December, specifically on New Year's Eve, I invited Maria to celebrate with us. It was a family tradition to spend New Year's Eve around my paternal grandmother's home so that she could give us her blessing when the clock struck twelve. But something was different. Due to the war that had just been won against Escobar, I felt a shift in the atmosphere; we were different, and I confirmed my suspicions when I overheard a conversation that my father was having with one of his accomplices.

"What do you wish for in this upcoming year?"

My father's answer made me understand what was going on: my father was starting to lose all sense of reality.

"Power. More power," he answered. This was the only thing he wished to attain in the year to come, and he said it with such certainty that I shivered.

I felt that my father was no longer the same. The humble men that had tried to live parallel lives between good and evil, while also attempting to amass a substantive fortune that they could later legitimize, were turning into something dangerously similar to that man that had met his end on the roof of a home in Medellín.

CHAPTER 6

During the late Forties, Colombian soccer went from being sensationally mediocre to being A-level due to the fact that soccer players in Argentina had gone on strike to fight for their rights. The soccer club Millonarios F.C. from Bogotá took advantage of the strike and offered deals to Adolfo Pedernera, to Néstor Rossi, and to Argentine soccer's promising star, Alfredo Di Stéfano. Alongside Colombian players, these men became part of one of the best teams in the world: the Millonarios de El Dorado.

The limited amount of regulations imposed by our government in respect to the formation of soccer teams served to turn our league into a sort of pirated league, which caught the attention of various soccer stars that left their countries to play in Colombian teams. The lawlessness that existed in the Colombian league brought about a period of growth for our soccer, known as "El Dorado." This era is remembered due to a game where Millonarios beat Real Madrid. Millonarios was considered the best team in the world.

In 1953, Colombia repaired her differences with FIFA and put an end to this pirated league. The soccer stars returned to their original teams, and our country went back to sustaining a mediocre level of soccer; only in 1978, with the Deportivo Cali, was Colombia able to make it to the final game in the Copa Libertadores de América. In regard to our national soccer team, we had only qualified for one World Cup in Chile during 1962, and had only been able to achieve getting crowned as the runner-up team during the Copa América that took place in Lima in 1975.

My biggest dream had been to become a professional soccer player. My father never allowed me to follow this dream. He had already planned out my future, and he had not envisioned me on a soccer field; instead, I was to become a high-level executive in his empire. Even with no support, I continued to fight for my dream and tried my luck at América's rival team.

Unfortunately, the players discriminated against me because I came from wealth and had access to the latest gear. The players that were part of a different social class were preferred. This generated a great feeling of anger in me: it was not my fault that I had access to more resources and I had not chosen to be born into my family. These kinds of injustices made my blood boil, and I ended up getting into a fight with the leader of the players. For this reason, I decided to give up on becoming a professional soccer player. I believed that what motivated me was different than what motivated the other players: My passion was soccer, theirs was finding a way out. So, I decided to focus my energy and my dreams on becoming an attorney.

Ever since he was a kid, my father had been a fan of América de Cali to the death. This was the common people's team, "La Mechita." The team that belonged to those that had nothing, and was said to have been cursed by fans to never win; for years, it was known as "the heart attack team": they either lost or won at the last minute.

In the late Seventies, everything changed for this modest institution. It went from being a sort of Cinderella to becoming the most important team in Colombia's history, recognized by FIFA in 1997 as the second-best team in the world, behind only Juventus of Italy.

In 1979, my father, tired from watching his beloved team lose, decided to approach this institution and told the board of directors that he, alongside some other fans, was more than willing to gift the soccer team three players. The board agreed: Juan Manuel Battaglia, Gonzalez Aquino, and Carlos Alfredo Gay came to the team's rescue.

With such a significant gift, Pepino Sangiovanni, América's president, was able to hire Mr. Gabriel Ochoa, a recognized soccer coach in Colombian soccer, a strategist of the most skilled kind. That same year, Ochoa led "La Mechita" to victory. The team managed to win its first national title for its suffering fans that had waited to taste the sweet nectar of victory for over fifty years.

The board of directors felt such immense gratitude that they invited the donors to become stakeholders and to hold leadership positions among the board. This is how Miguel Rodríguez went on to become this humble institution's newest sponsor. My father invested large quantities of money in the team, which made the hiring of all-star players, like Willington Ortiz, Ricardo Gareca, Roberto Cabañas, Julio César Uribe, César Cueto, and many more, possible.

Due to this influx of capital and leadership, América was able to win five titles in the domestic championship during the Eighties; plus, they made it three times to the finals in the Copa Libertadores de América, the most respected tournament in the continent. Many drew links between the inability to win this tournament with the "curse" or blamed the team's mascot, a devil, but these were just myths that provided excuses for the fans, not for the directors. They knew that every defeat came as a result of a tactical error, not as a result of some dark magic.

At first, my father was in charge of directing the team to the satisfaction of a fan base that was unfamiliar with the taste of victory, but, when he started to notice the power and influence that came with his new role, he changed. People would do anything to get a ticket, and being in the stadium watching your team in a final match was the ultimate reward. All the telephones at América's headquarters rang incessantly. Everyone, from a simple citizen to the mayor, wanted to get their envelope of tickets.

Understanding this, my father used soccer to build relationships within the high social spheres of Colombia. He was a pioneer amongst a group of men, in the Eighties, that took advantage of a certain niche that the State and the private sector had left open, and invested large sums of drug-trafficking money, which led to the development of a higher level of soccer in Colombia.

This boom led to a flourishing of national soccer similar to that of the "El Dorado" era. Important foreign players began to see Colombia's soccer scene with different eyes and, next to the new national superstars, managed to make our league competitive. As the league became competitive, national players had to try harder, and new stars emerged, like Carlos "Pibe" Valderrama, Freddy Rincon, Faustino Asprilla, and others that were at the center of what I call "the Second Dorado." During this particular era, our country experienced many great achievements, like qualifying for three World Cups.

Society, content with its new-found victory, accepted an emerging social group that invested dirty money into various sectors of the economy, especially in sports. And, in this manner, they welcomed the benefits that these investments created for them, specifically for those people and institutions that had legally constructed their businesses.

In a similar manner, everyone that got involved in soccer searched for, aside from personal satisfaction, recognition. Many people began to believe that administering a team was a simple task. Being the head of a successful multinational company did not mean that you would easily be able to attain a win. Soccer is a business that has many unpredictable variables: players' egos, their financial needs, their mental well-being, the fan base, etc. These factors that lay outside the realm of the simply physical are contingencies that need to be understood in order to be able to guide a team in difficult situations, which requires you to spend all of your time surrounded by many advisors that can help guide you to victory.

My father had Pepino Sangiovanni and Mr. Gabriel Ochoa to teach him the ropes. I had him. He taught me how to deal with players, a fundamental skill when it comes to getting anything accomplished. I learned that in order to expect results, I needed to follow through with whatever I said.

When I decided to get involved in América, in 1989, I did it with a revolutionary purpose: I wanted to turn a team that depended on buying and bringing in players and that had neglected the development of the young players in their own ranks because they had access to my father's checkbook, which had been used to buy and sign the best players in the country, into a team that could produce their own stars at home. This was not an easy mission. The team was used to winning and did not have faith in the young players that usually debuted aged around twenty. Nonetheless, I structured and led a committee of prosperous businessmen with whom I began working on applying a certain model that had been used to achieve great victory during the Eighties by a team from Holland, Ajax.

This model consisted of reinforcing the inferior divisions by working on their technical strategy, their physique, their mental health, and their nutrition so that true talent could be discovered. Once they were discovered, they were sent to play abroad so that the players could integrally develop as people and professionals.

We were pioneers in the field of minor leagues. I knew that the bubble created by easy access to dirty money would eventually pop due to the war that was being waged directly against drug trafficking. Sooner or later, my father would not be able to continue providing economic assistance to the team. Believing that the only way to salvage the team was to make sure it was self-sufficient, I dedicated my body and soul to this purpose, simultaneously exorcizing the frustration I harbored because I had not carried out my dream of becoming a professional player.

As director of the development of the minor leagues, I visualized the team as national champions. I was able to achieve this dream six years later, just within the time range that I had predicted.

The first thing I did was to replace the coaching staff. I searched the market for the best in player development so that I could strengthen the sub-seventeen squad, and, in 1992, placing all my hopes and efforts in these young men, I organized a tournament called "El Torneo de la Esperanza." I tested them out against foreign teams like Real Madrid, River Plate, Flamengo...

This tournament went on for many years, giving our players the exposure that they needed to gain experience so that they could make it to the professional first team. Thanks to this effort, players like Frankie Oviedo, Jairo Castillo, Gerson González, and Leonardo Moreno were forged.

At the beginning of 1994, due to the persecution that my father was undergoing at the hands of the Colombian government and foreign nations, he gave me control over the professional team; I was surprised because the men I had been grooming were not prepared to take on the pressure of carrying the team on their backs. The professional first team had players that were recognized internationally like Jorge Bermúdez, Antony de Ávila, Leonel Álvarez, Óscar Córdoba, and many more.

Nonetheless, I assumed command and that year we fought hard for a championship title that was taken from us by a suspicious decision made by the referee in Medellín. I did not give up, and, the next year, I structured a team that was even better, but the same referee, this time in Barranquilla, stole the cup from us again, allowing two offside goals to count. That day I realized that, in soccer, having a good team is not enough; you must have the man in black on your side, as referees are the ones that, in the final minutes, can define a game.

In 1995, my father was captured. These were terrible times for the entire family and for the institution my father and uncle had built. The weekly migration of our entire family from Cali to Bogotá had a huge cost, not only because of the cost of plane tickets, but also the effort that it required; we needed time, willingness, zest, and, above all, it required a tremendous logistical operation to keep us safe in Cali and in Bogotá—there were new threats from emerging organizations from which my father and uncle needed to keep us safe. For this reason, I was not especially worried about the fact that my father would become unable to provide economic support to América de Cali. Our circumstances were so dire that one day my aunt Amparo, who was in charge of the administrative side of things at América, said to me, "Son, we don't even have enough money to buy coffee."

"Don't worry about it, Aunt Amparo. We will get out of this; we just need to sell some players that have completed their time here," I said to her, while I looked her straight in the eyes and thought about the amazing job she was doing as administrator.

That we didn't even have enough money for coffee reflected the state the team was in. Our pockets were empty, not because the money had been administered incorrectly, but because soccer is more than a business, it's a passion that can give you everything but can also take it away.

The calmness with which I reassured my aunt stemmed from an offer that I had received from Bavaria, from a business that wanted to pay us a million dollars for our uniform. Plus, we had qualified for Copa Libertadores, which meant that we would be making more money.

I knew that this was the perfect moment to make my dream of turning América into a team that was self-sufficient by selling the more experienced players and forming, with the emerging talents, a strong group that would put up a good fight for the Copa Libertadores. The emergence of some of the players that I had been training from the minor leagues was extremely helpful as they served as reinforcements for the more mature players.

Once again, we were deeply disillusioned because we lost the cup. We had been close, but, once again, we had made a mistake in the final stages. People said that luck had been against us, but luck is just an excuse used by those who are not capable. I knew that I had made a mistake picking the captain of our ship, and it was time to look for a winning coach. I decided to hire Luis Augusto "Chiqui" García, a man that had started out training the minor leagues of Millonarios, and that, later, with the professional first team, had gone on to win two national championships in 1987 and 1988.

Initially, the decision I made to bring him to América de Cali caused some friction between me and my father. He had a troubled history with "El Chiqui." He associated him with the majority shareholder of Millonarios, Gonzalo Rodríguez Gacha, who had been Pablo Escobar's associate in the Medellín Cartel, and had been an enemy during the war against him. But, to my surprise, even though he had his doubts, he gave me permission. I think that my father's decision to allow Chiqui to come work at América was influenced by a certain guilt that my father carried over what had happened to me. Meaning that thanks to the attempt on my life, Luis Augusto was able to coach the team.

From the start, there was a certain chemistry between me and Garcia. We spoke the same language; he saw soccer as a business made up of five-year cycles that were used to drive players to their peak performance before then selling them in their prime. Most directors would become fascinated by a certain player and would allow the player to turn old among the team's ranks, putting a stop to the formative cycle in the minor leagues; this way, you would never make back what you had spent on the player. It's like a circus: if you don't change the clowns, the performance will soon go out of style because audiences will get bored and stop coming to the show.

We built an amazing team. For this campaign, we had a solid foundation, and that team that I had created five years prior in the minor leagues was ready to take on an unthinkable feat for América: to become champions with over 80% of the players made at home.

That year, the Colombian teams fought for the title in the longest tournament in the history of Colombian soccer. It took a year and a half for the new champions to be crowned, a decision that was made from Medellín by my rival at the time, Nacional. Nacional had a lot of influence due to sponsorships, but I was no longer the innocent boy from 1994, when I had lost a league due to unsportsmanlike decisions. Now I knew what it meant to manipulate the strings of influence, and I was prepared to do whatever was necessary.

With García at the helm, we had the best campaign in the history of América de Cali, winning fifteen consecutive games. As a result of this campaign, and for having made it to the Copa

Libertadores final, in 1997, we were ranked as the second-best team in the world by FIFA, something that filled Colombia with pride and satiated the thirst of América's dedicated fan base.

Our triumph in the championship was a sure thing, but, once again, an invisible hand tried to undermine our hard work. Halfway through the tournament, the federation modified the rules, arguing that we needed to have two champions per year. A star was to be given out every six months due to financial necessity.

When I saw that the federation had managed to get the votes necessary to implement this, I moved heaven and earth to make sure that the number one team of the year had a guaranteed spot in the final. I got what I wanted. América was first, which meant that their spot in the final was secured.

During those six months, we dedicated our efforts to carefully preparing for that final, while the other teams wore themselves down in order to make it. We had to face Bucaramanga, a province that had had an amazing campaign and left our usual rivals out of the competition.

Everything was aligned so that we could achieve what we had been tirelessly working toward for five years. We won our ninth star, making my dream of crowning América as champions with a team composed mostly of players raised in our own ranks. This was all thanks to an executive board that had been willing to find the money we needed to motivate this spectacular group of players, a coach with a winning spirit like Chiqui García, and the unconditional support of the best fans. The entire América family felt an overwhelming joy that we had been able to, once again, reach the top of the national league. The best result was the economic well-being that befell on the team.

I traveled to Bogotá to see my father and dedicate this triumph to him. Deep down, I wanted him to recognize my efforts, but instead, he welcomed me with news that felt like a bucket of ice had been thrown on me. He would not support the continuance of Chiqui as head coach. He had wrongly decided to support another faction of the executive board, one that my aunt was a part of, that wanted to get rid of García.

Disillusioned and with my morale at rock bottom, I told him that I would return to dealing with the minor leagues, and that he could, alongside his sister, take care of the professional first team. I was not going to accept the hiring of Francisco Maturana as head coach, and I got my way. When Maturana called me to see if it was true that the team was interested in him, I told him he did not stand a chance, so he made the smart decision to back down and let other coaches have their shot.

After Maturana turned them down, the board decided to name Diego Umaña as head coach. This was a mistake. Umaña had been by my side during my first years at the institution, and we had failed; it was just a matter of time until he failed again. I dedicated my time to planning the team for the next cycle of five years, looking to reinforce our bases once again.

Thanks to some advice by Fernando Velasco, a dear friend, I met a young coach named Jaime de la Pava that was building a successful career among the minor leagues. I liked the way he approached the world of soccer and hired him to lead our third division. That year, we won the national championship in our category, a reality that hinted at a bright future.

Unfortunately, the professional team failed and coach Umaña retired in November of 1998, before the tournament was even over. He was replaced by young coach de la Pava.

My father requested that I meet him in Bogotá, at his new detainment center, in order to discuss who would be placed in the role as head coach for the next season. He wanted to bring in someone with a high profile, but due to the team's failure, we did not have the resources to do so. He asked my opinion, and I told him he should hire Jaime de la Pava. Even though he had his doubts, he ended up agreeing to hire him.

I met with coach de la Pava so that we could develop a strategy for what was sure to be a difficult season. Our players had an average age of twenty-three, and most of them had emerged from the lower divisions of América. This fact suggested to us that this could be the most difficult campaign yet: the players and the coach lacked experience. I told myself that I would make sure that we succeeded, and I drilled this into the minds of everyone, from the board, to the team, to the employees ... I even made sure that the lady that made our coffee knew the words, "Victory and victory, only." This would not only bring triumph to the team, but it would be financially beneficial for all the players.

To achieve this goal, it was necessary that we secured two things: the money to pay the players' salaries and bonuses, and, secondly, the banishment of a certain referee that had ruled against us in the past. The board complied with the first requirement. To make sure we could get the second, I went to Bogotá and met with the federation to let them know that I did not want "the best referee" to be placed in any of América's games. I was able to make sure that he was never in charge of our games due to the past calls that he had made against us. Being able to reassure my players, whom I had instilled with the idea that we would win, that the odds would not be skewed against them, brought them a great sense of tranquility.

Effectively, we managed to win the first international triumph in our history: La Copa Merconorte. Plus, we managed to make it to the final in the national championship, where we lost to Medellín on penalties. Overall, it was a positive balance that allowed us to solidify a group of players and a coach that had bright futures in the world of soccer.

We all looked toward the new millennium with a lot of hope. I tried to analyze where we had gone wrong that season. I decided that I needed to strengthen three positions: I brought in Luis Barbat as goalie, Luis Garcia as a central midfielder, and Julián Vázquez as forward. These players added the level of experience that the team needed and helped us win our tenth star, to the satisfaction of an entire city and fandom.

I had managed to instill in the players the only thing that is essential to winning: the taste for victory. I turned América into a well-oiled machine destined for victory; in 2001, we were once again national champions. Two months before the final, I met with coach de la Pava and, together, we arrived at the conclusion that it was necessary that he take a year off at the end of the season. Soccer is ever-changing, and, in order to keep up, you must be constantly evolving, just like in any other field, to continue being successful.

But, one more time, my father got in my way. He did not share my opinion and went over my head to convince de la Pava to stay for one more season. That was the last straw. I could not continue tolerating the constant disrespect from a person that was not even part of the day-to-day dealings of team matters, and that, in my opinion, continued to make decisions that went against the well-being of the institution. I wrote him a letter irrevocably resigning from my position, and wrote in it some words that I believe hurt him deeply: "América does not belong to anyone, it is a passion that lives ingrained in our heart, and it belongs to all of us."

This was the legacy I left behind in the world of soccer. I worked tirelessly for the well-being of a team. I never received a single dollar for my efforts and built a structure aimed toward the future. If they had followed the blueprint, they would have continued to triumph the way they had when I was there. But today, I look at what has become of my beloved "machita" with profound sadness.

Those that came after me looked only to satisfy their own personal interests, not those of the organization. I found their excuses to be trivial. They blamed the Clinton list or the "blacklist" created in 1995 by the Office of Foreign Affairs of the United States' Department of the Treasury, where many businesses and people that had benefitted from drug money were listed. I had dealt with that list and never let it come between me and the goal of bringing triumph to the hearts of our fans. Under my administration, which was quite lucrative from an economic point of view, we were national champions four times, won the Copa Merconorte, came second in the Copa Libertadores once, and managed second place twice in the national tournament.

CHAPTER 7

It wasn't really a secret that the Cali Cartel, with its leadership and financial assistance, had played a huge part in bringing down the Medellín Cartel. It had financed the Search Bloc; gathered and shared vital intelligence on Pablo; and had donated machinery that was used to intercept and locate phone calls, etc. Furthermore, the Cali Cartel had paid the rewards that had been offered for the take down of Escobar, "El Mexicano," and the large majority of his accomplices.

During the war, I had graduated as an attorney. I had clear intentions to open my own practice, which would, I imagined, help me to get my career in the world of litigation started, preparing me for future battles that I would have to confront to maintain my family's judicial stability. My father and uncle had begun negotiations that would prove transcendental for their future.

God places opportunities in front of us, but only we have the power to decide whether or not to take them. My father and uncle had everything in their favor to turn themselves into the authorities and resolve their legal troubles through the judicial system. Many sectors of Colombian society felt a deep sense of gratitude toward them because of their role in Escobar's demise.

At the beginning of 1994, they began reaching out to the attorney general at the time, Gustavo de Greiff, in what was described as the subjugation of the Cali Cartel to the Colombian government. The government was interested in turning the page on this horrible chapter, not only to uphold peace in the country, but because of the pressure they were under from the American government that desperately wanted the cartel's bosses behind bars.

This negotiation was doomed from the start. Neither side was actually seriously considering reaching a mutually beneficial agreement. My father and uncle had completely lost their grip on reality. They thought they were invincible after having achieved two impossible feats: getting my uncle extradited to Colombia and not the United States like the Gringos wanted, and the fall of the Medellín Cartel. It is not hard to understand why their egos were inflated, and, walking on a cloud, they mistakenly believed that they could overcome whatever obstacles got in their way. Their power blinded them and that is what doomed them: they truly believed that they were above the law. They let the best opportunity that our family ever had to resolve our legal issues once and for all slip by.

The first offer that they made was unacceptable in the eyes of the authorities: they wanted to be placed under house arrest, something that was unfathomable due to the embarrassment faced by the government after letting Pablo stay in La Catedral. Their requests were so far-fetched that they quickly exhausted the government's patience and that of an honest man like Mr. De Greiff.

Political power is unpredictable, and it is constantly changing hands. César Gaviria aspired to become the new Secretary General of the United States' Organization (OEA), and to do this, he needed the approval and support of the North American government, which is why he could not offer the Rodríguez brothers any sort of special treatment. Plus, the Cali Cartel had become the new target of the US State Department in the war against drugs.

In August 1991, the ship *Mercader del Continente* reached the ports in Miami. The former agent of the DEA, Edward Kacerosky, was in charge of intercepting shipments sent to Miami during this time. When they searched the ship, they found numerous columns and stones filled with cocaine. There were twelve tons of cocaine on that ship, an amount that was worth 200 million dollars on US soil. Under Kacerosky's orders, they let the shipment go through with the intention of staying on its trail. After capturing various men in Texas, they initiated the largest investigation against drug trafficking and money laundering carried out by the United States government: Operation *Cornerstone*. From that moment forward, Special Agent Kacerosky, a man with a Polish background that loved art and basketball, began a persecution against the Cali Cartel that knew no limits. He wanted to show the world that this organization was just as powerful as the Medellín Cartel, and that it currently controlled, according to his information, 80% of the drug market in the United States.

As Kacerosky continued to approach, my father and uncle, due to their own human conditions, fell victim to a trap created by illustrious and intelligent men in the political sphere that, like vermin, managed to get them on an imaginary pedestal and made them believe that they could help them solve all of their issues politically, something that never happened.

In those tempestuous moments, I returned from completing a Master's in Business and Marketing at the Business Institute of Madrid, and turned my focus to developing my legal practice, which achieved fruitful results due to my father's many connections in the judicial sphere. I began inheriting these powerful connections thanks to the knowledge my father had given me that taught me how to manipulate a sector of our government that has been consumed by corruption: "Everything can be solved if you know the right people or have access to the amount of money necessary to buy someone's conscience," he told me.

I had started to taste the sweet but dangerous nectar that came with power that, like a narcotic, enters your bloodstream and slowly begins infecting your conscience. Due to the difficult position that my father was in, he began delegating certain jobs that fell under the legal realm to me like managing the soccer team, the real estate businesses, and the various processes that had been initiated against our family.

Slowly but surely, I started to become an important piece in his world, something that filled me with happiness, but, when I observed his attitude, it filled me with sadness: the more things I did right, the less he seemed to acknowledge. Maybe it was his own way of preparing me to be the best. This was the situation that I found myself in when I received surprising news.

During these difficult years, Maria had always remained by my side. Patiently, she waited for me to finish my studies, to travel, to learn, to experiment, with the certainty that I would return to her. For her, our relationship was a serious one, not really because of the compromise but more because it took a certain level of understanding to maintain due to the type of person that I was. She was the one that always came to visit me at home, not because she wanted to, but for my safety—something that I will always thank her for because, even though she knew the danger that this could put her in due to my father's many enemies, she never faltered. She also had to withstand a period of my life that I refer to as "senseless," a product of the illusion of power that money creates and of the adrenaline that came with it: a lethal cocktail that always brings negative consequences with it.

When Maria told me that she was pregnant, my world turned 180 degrees. This event made me rethink what I was doing with my life, not because of the pregnancy, for this brought me immense joy, but because I realized that my life had become what my father and my family wanted, what everyone else wanted; I never thought about myself—I was simply a cog in a machine.

I had dedicated my life to imitating those of others inside of an empty, bohemian atmosphere, where I was being consumed by alcohol and pleasure. When I learned that I was going to be a father, I realized that I was no longer a boy, that I had to take on the new role that life had given me in earnest; and I began to take notice of the positive aspects of marriage.

I remembered how much I craved a family unit when my parents got a divorce, and to me, Maria was the true embodiment of a good woman, with good principles and who was intelligent. Convinced that she was the woman with whom I wanted to spend the rest of my life, I made a decision based on the genuine love that I felt for her and on the hope that my daughter would have the family that I never did. I knew how important it was to have a loving father and mother that worried about your well-being.

My mother-in-law, a woman with pristine principles who I admire deeply, in spite of her stern yet noble character, was vehemently opposed to my proposal. I had asked Maria to move in with me. In that moment, she turned to me with that air of tranquility and poise that characterizes her and answered, "If moving in is what you are offering, I would prefer to continue living with my family."

Raised with good manners and values, she demonstrated, once again, the admirable woman that she was. She would not abandon her home if we were not married in the eyes of God. This revelation gave me the strength I needed to take the leap. I was sure that Maria was, and she is, the best woman that I could share my life with, and this way, we could secure a family for our baby.

The next step was to speak with my father. I went to visit him in one of the houses where he was hiding. Sitting at the small table in the corridor, where he usually welcomed people that provided him with information and from where he conducted his business—this is what his office had turned into—he told me, to my surprise, that he considered Maria to be a great woman. He also said that he was delighted to hear this, that she was happy that she would be my wife.

Having made my decision, I went home and told my aunt Mariela what I had decided. She saw the news in such a positive light that all she did was give me a hug filled with love and affection. She told me that this was the right choice. The next day, with a ring in my hand, I was in front of Mrs. Emma, asking for her daughter's hand in marriage.

On our wedding day, as I was exiting my room dressed in my suit, my aunt Mariela stopped and stared me up and down. I thought there was something wrong with my suit. But after that initial reaction, she said something that maybe she had dreamt up for me, words that I will never forget: "Marriage is a responsibility that must be taken on with love, it is nothing more." Then, she blessed me and suggested that I leave any childish uncertainties behind so that I could make decisions like an adult.

I left the apartment with a profound sadness because I knew that I would never return there as someone who lived in that home that had given me so much love. My bodyguards were waiting for me at the entrance of the building. In the church called Santa Teresita, the place where our wedding would take place and our union would be sanctified, I saw both of our families: my grandmother, who walked me down the aisle; my cousins; and my friends. My father and uncle were not there: it would have been too risky for them to be there.

We went to the reception in a BMW. We moved through the border of the city as we contemplated Cali's beautiful sunset, which only made this moment even more romantic. We recounted our courtship, we remembered the day that we had met on campus, we reflected on the good and bad things that we had been through, we even narrated the progression of the party. It was an exciting moment, filled with anticipation about what our future would really hold.

The security systems were up and running. From the heart of the Search Bloc, we were being kept up to date on any kind of movement of troops being made. We also had someone informing us from the airport, from a shed that was near to the National Police headquarters, and from the military. The persecution that was being carried out against my father and uncle was in full steam, which would turn my wedding into the last big party by the Cali Cartel where the big bosses were in attendance. A party with over 200 guests that was planned, according to them, to honor the new couple.

Invitations had not been sent out until the day before, just to follow through with the formality of invitations and to reassure the guests that the event was indeed going to take place. The invitations had one peculiarity: they had no address. It was a matter of security. The day of the wedding, guests were to arrive to a specific location, and only then would the actual location of the event be disclosed to them.

Various security rings were established to ensure the safety and security of my father and uncle, who had not been able to attend the ceremony due to their current circumstances. The way to the venue—which was the club El Remanso—and all of the access routes to the location, were completely controlled by my father's security team. It was a beautiful place on the outskirts of town, where my father had built a grand party hall to hold his events.

It was a strategic point due to its geographical location. In case of a necessary evacuation, it had two paths through fields of cane and forests that were perfect for the movement of motorcycles in case of a rushed exit.

The party began after we had welcomed in various characters. My father gave a moving speech, and the night went by with almost no incidents, enlivened by various orchestras, foreshadowing that these times would change and that perhaps we would never experience anything like them again. The level of luxury was unusual and unlike my father's and uncle's personalities, who had always been moderate when it came to parties.

Because I have a sharp gift for observation, in the middle of the party, I realized that this party was not for me, and much less was it to celebrate the decision I had made to marry Maria. It was for my father! And, like in the movie *The Godfather*, everyone stopped to pay their respects to the Don first, instead of congratulating us who were supposedly being honored. I realized that the party, the orchestras, the champagne, the food were not there in celebration of our union, but were instead meant to show off the power and wealth of the Cali Cartel. This realization, mixed with the alcohol that I had consumed, boiled my blood and we got into an argument that, although quickly stopped by my aunt Mariela, showcased the level of delusion under which my father and uncle were living.

At five in the morning, I made my way to the Intercontinental

Hotel, where I would spend my wedding night. Leaving all arguments behind, we gave ourselves over to a beautiful sunrise, in which only the sun and the love I felt for Maria existed. I was unaware that a strong, threatening wind was blowing from the North due to the pressure that was being put on the Colombian government by the United States to capture my father and uncle.

CHAPTER 8

The first attempt by the Colombian justice system to capture the leaders of the Cali Cartel was a total failure. The men in charge of carrying out this immense task were, one way or another, connected to my father and uncle. The reason for these relationships was the recent war with Pablo Escobar.

Seeing that nothing was really being accomplished, the governments of Colombia and the United States decided to change their strategy. Under American influence, the National Police promoted to general, Rosso José Serrano, who had made a promise to the US that he would bring down the Cali Cartel. Ernesto Samper, a president whose reign had been tainted due to the scandal surrounding the "8,000 Process," had no say in the matter and had to submit to all of Washington's demands. In a wise move, Serrano named the sons of retired generals to positions of power in the National Police knowing that it would be a lot harder for the cartel to bribe and corrupt them.

This is how the "hombres grises" or "gray men," the sons of retired generals that were just getting their careers started, appeared on the scene—some of these men still hold important positions inside Colombia's National Police Force today. Under Serrano's command, the government carried out a ruthless persecution against my entire family to put pressure on my father and uncle, hoping that they would turn themselves in. The police carried out raids of our homes on a regular basis; my office was raided every two weeks approximately. The whole situation felt more like theatrics in order to intimidate us—the men carried big weapons and had their faces painted as they searched for any intel that I might have. They never found anything because I never had what they were looking for in the first place.

Due to the constant violation of my clients' privacy, I was forced to shut my office down: who would, in their right minds, want someone whose office was being raided by police every fifteen days as their legal representative? The same thing went on inside our homes. The police did not care whether children were present or not; it was just something that we had to deal with because we were members of the Rodríguez Orejuela family. The only thing that mattered to them was to carry out their strategy of putting pressure on us, making us desperate enough to get my uncle and father to turn themselves in.

The only thing that actually ended up working for them was the rewards they offered and the information that they got through informants. In Colombia, no one really falls due to the intelligence gathered by organizations, they fall because someone turns them in.

In 1994, Cali could still be controlled through a pretty simple security scheme: a network of informants, monitoring communications, and through some friends positioned in strategic places. It was relatively easy to carry out counterintelligence tasks and to know well ahead of time where police would raid next.

Radio stations, newspapers, and televised news were all used to advertise the monetary rewards being offered for the capture of the four leaders of the cartel, including my father and uncle. In the announcements, they publicized the numbers that were to be called if anyone had any information. The men in charge of counterintelligence, who worked for my father and uncle and were under the command of Major Del Vasto, intercepted those lines, analyzed the risks, and reported their analysis directly to their bosses. My uncle and father were the only ones allowed to make any kind of decisions regarding their movements. The level of infiltration was so deep that we always knew exactly what places were going to be raided ahead of time—the exact time, place, and agents in charge—and were able to effectively distribute this information to everyone in the organization so that those in danger could change location or hide.

An event that we are still unable to explain involving Guillermo Pallomari, the former accountant for the cartel, occurred. Pallomari was a Chilean that had become an integral piece in the cartel's structure due to his extensive knowledge and training as a systems engineer. On that day, my father called him to tell him that his office was to be raided, yet, to everyone's surprise, he chose to stay there with a briefcase that contained all of the cartel's accounts. The information in that briefcase would serve as a starting point for a case aimed at punishing all of the political class that had sold their consciences to the cartel and had benefitted from millions of dollars over several years. That case was the "8,000 Process," which was used by the country's attorney general, Alfonso Valdivieso Sarmiento.

As a result of their failed attempts in phase two and due to mounting US pressure, the government—led by Rosso José Serrano—changed its strategy. The Americans contributed more money, which, in turn, let them raise the monetary rewards for the capture of any of the four cartel bosses. Due to this change, I was unable to see my father for three months, until, one day, I was told by his most trusted men that he needed me.

When we met, he asked me to interview an attorney in Bogotá that had told him about the possibility of an action for protection, as described in Article 86 of the Colombian Constitution that gives citizens the right to protect the basic constitutional rights of an individual, against the numerous television ads, where their photos were constantly shared, because they violated the protection of their reputation and one or another fundamental right.

Effectively, and because only we had the right to present that petition—my grandmother, due to her rights as a mother, and me, due to my rights as a son—I accepted this mission and presented my request to the Judicial Circuit in Bogotá. The judgment was in our favor, and the transmission of ads was suspended.

This result led to a penal investigation against my father, who was constantly heard by the authorities due to their investigative technology, but was unable to be located. He used a unique system of encryptions that would only be discovered after his arrest. Thoughtlessly, he mentioned the name of a certain judge that had made some sort of deal with him for a positive result to my action for protection request. This phone call was used to start the investigation.

Even after we got the win in the courts, which ended up turning me into a main player, I had to show up in court to state my innocence in the supposed coercion.

In the meantime, Jorge Salcedo—ironically, the son of a retired general—who was in charge of the communication within the Cali Cartel, began to realize that this ship was sinking, so he engineered a Machiavellian scheme to hand my father to the authorities, and thus, he began his treasonous plan.

Because he was merely in charge of communications, he did not have access to the inner security rings or to the information that was necessary in order to capture the leaders of the cartel. After the incident in Costa Rica, where two "papaya" bombs were confiscated, my uncle Gilberto, who gave Salcedo his post due to his experience and knowledge in communications, began to lose his trust in him.

Salcedo had made a deal with the American authorities to turn in the four leaders of the cartel or to do whatever was necessary to stop the cartel, but he did not have the means to. The constant pressure from the Americans put him in a tight position, so, he decided to turn his friend in, Major Mario del Vasto, a man who was loyal to the cartel and that spearheaded my dad's security.

The strategy consisted in gaining Mario del Vasto's trust in order to familiarize himself with his movements. When Salcedo learned that he was to carry out training of some of his men in the south of Cali, he contacted his new allies. These mounted an impressive operation that led to the major's capture along with twelve men that were with him. They were accused of being part of Miguel Rodríguez's security team, and of benefitting from dirty money. This was a master strategy that had been orchestrated by the Americans, making it obvious that they were the ones responsible for my dad's chase and capture, not the infamous intelligence reports being handed in by General Serrano.

On one occasion, due to a fight with his wife, my father decided to not go visit her in a certain apartment near Granada in the north of Cali, where they met up whenever possible. Jorge Salcedo knew of these secret meetings, and he happened to mention this particular one to his new American allies. Luck was on my father's side, though, as he only sent a vehicle with a couple of items to the apartment. The authorities waited until the car was in the garage, and, at one in the morning, they raided the apartment and found that their attempt had failed.

After this raid, my dad began taking extraordinary precautions. Noticing that he was vulnerable, he completely isolated himself and kept the need for big moves to a minimum. My uncle Gilberto, on the other hand, had a security detail that was completely different. One of his main men made the mistake of allowing a childhood friend to move into his house in Cali, in order to help him combat addiction. My uncle's assistant, El Flaco, would thoughtlessly mention things about his work to his friend. His friend began to deduce who his friend's possible boss was and informed the authorities immediately. The police trailed El Flaco all the way to his office in the north of Cali, which is near the main branch of the Carvajal Company, a well-known Colombian company.

This area was particularly secure. To access it, there were steep stairs, and there was only one way to enter, which made it easy to locate anyone that did not belong there. Due to this inconvenience, the police enlisted a special group of officers made up of young women that frequented this area for training to watch El Flaco and track his moves until they found the exact building that he was entering. They planned the operation on the morning of a Friday and, in the afternoon that same day, they raided the home: my uncle was captured on June 9, 1995.

The fact that my uncle's capture had been due to information provided by another person worried Jorge Salcedo, who had not only failed to deliver on the promises he made to the North American agencies, but also worried that he would not receive the reward, which was ultimately the one thing he really cared about. So, he decided to focus all of his energy into capturing his boss, Miguel Rodríguez.

In his desperation over his brother's capture, my father called upon Salcedo for a meeting, where he asked Salcedo for his help in evading capture and raids. Salcedo saw the perfect opportunity to mend the trust that had been broken and offered him his help, keeping his one true objective in mind: turning him in and claiming the reward.

Only a few days after my uncle's arrest, Salcedo learned that my father was staying in a house in Santa Mónica Residencial, an exclusive neighborhood in the north of Cali. With the exact address in hand, as he had left my father there just a couple of minutes earlier, he ordered his wife to inform the authorities.

My father had hired another man known as Pinchaito, who was in charge of giving him the tapes that had the communications of the Search Bloc on them. My father received a tape that contained the phone call that gave them his exact address at 1 p.m., so he immediately ordered the house to be cleared and evacuated. The Search Bloc got there at 2.30 p.m. Once again, my father had evaded capture, but a question remained: who was the informant that had turned him in?

Still reeling from the latest raid, my father moved to an apartment in the neighborhood known as Santa Rita, located on the west side of Cali, where he remained hidden for ten days. Jorge Salcedo knew the area, but he did not know which building my father was in, until, one day, my father made the mistake of asking Salcedo to drop him off in said building's garage. With my father's exact location in hand, Salcedo informed the Search Bloc again.

The new operation was planned carefully, and it even included the involvement of General Serrano. Serrano, confident in the information provided by the DEA, told his pilot, a captain that reported to my father, that they were headed to carry out an operation in Tulua. This captain told my father where General Serrano was dead, which calmed his nerves. But what he didn't realize then was that they could reach him from Tulua. The Search Bloc positioned its men in the Portada del Mar, an entryway to the city that leads to Buenaventura, and, from there, they moved on foot until they reached the building in Santa Rita, which was about a kilometer away.

The Special Forces entered the building at 5.30 p.m. My father, aware of the presence of the authorities, hid in a nearly undetectable "caleta," or hiding place. The men raided every single apartment and found his secretary on the second floor, which led them to search the building again, inch by inch.

In the meantime, having learned of what was going on, Nicol and Dario, who was the second in command when it came to my father's security detail, informed me of what was occurring. We decided to meet somewhere near the raid, so we met up in a cafeteria in the Centenario neighborhood. There, I called upon Jorge Salcedo, not before ordering men to monitor the perimeter five to ten blocks out. I needed to know what was going on and to figure out how we could help my father.

The desperation among the Special Forces men was so great that they brought in engineers to figure out where it was possible to find a "caleta." During their efforts, they used heavy machinery to bring down walls, and one man gravely injured his hand with a saw.

It was almost 6 p.m. Dario called me over and told me about the suspicions he had about Jorge Salcedo, who, in a panic, came and went over and over again to our meeting spot. This suspicious behavior, plus Dario's comments, led me to distrust him. So, when he came back to where we were stationed, I told him my father had been able to escape, and that he was safe—a lie. Salcedo immediately informed the Special Forces of this, and they suspended the operation, which saved my father.

To those of us that had been in that small cafeteria, it was evident who the traitor was. It was a serious situation.

"What should we do, boss? Should I put him in a coffin?" asked Nicol.

I thought about it, but I immediately faltered. I was not used to making decisions about people's lives. I think that in that millisecond, I made the best decision of my life.

I turned to Nicol and said, "Don't worry about it. My father will decide what to do with that asshole."

In order to escape the building, my father called upon a sergeant that was in the Special Forces, who he referred to as "Martha," to survey the building and come up with an exit strategy. At first, Martha offered to take him in the trunk of his car, but this idea was quickly shut down due to the fact that every vehicle that entered or left the building was checked. The only way out was to get through a wall that was almost three meters tall and bordered the mountains. At the crack of dawn, with the help of Martha and two other men, my father went over the wall and walked for a couple of hours in the wild until he reached one of his wife's apartments.

That same day, I informed him through Dario what we had deduced about Jorge Salcedo, but he, in a crazed trance, refused to believe us. According to him, Salcedo was a loyal man that had stuck by our side during the war with Medellín.

Jorge Salcedo met with my father in his wife's apartment, and they planned his move to an apartment in the building Hacienda Buenos Aires, where my father would finally be captured.

Once my father was in the new building, the North American agents contacted Salcedo. Upset, they demanded that he deliver my father immediately or he would lose all the benefits they had agreed upon. Salcedo asked them for a week, telling them that he was gathering information so that they could also confiscate a large sum of money.

Eight days later, they planned a new operation sure that the information provided by Jorge Salcedo was accurate. General Serrano made up a celebration for a group of policemen to prevent any informants from getting wind of the situation, and, in the morning, on August 6, 1995, the operation that would lead to my father's capture began.

Our watchmen that were stationed outside of the building did not notice the Special Forces arrive, as they approached the building through the mountainous terrain at the back. Once they were in the building, they blew up the door so that my father would not have time for anything. They had learned, through Salcedo, about the perfection of his "caletas," or hiding places.

After the explosion, my father grabbed a bag with the intention of hiding in his caleta, but his wife asked him not to, as she believed they would kill him. He was arrested in his room. The theatrics continued in Bogotá with interviews and celebrations. That same day, he was transferred to La Picota, where my uncle, who had been there for two months, was anxiously waiting for him.

It was a tough blow for all of us, but it was also a relief for many of us, as well. We had received information that suggested that the Search Block had been growing impatient and were willing to kill them just to stop them. Those moments were filled with anguish and despair because the ship was left with no captain. The next day, I got a call from my father; he wanted me to fly to Bogotá. I left immediately and was able to see him due to my license as an attorney.

It was an emotional meeting—we were both sad—because, even though we always knew that he was at risk, we never imagined that this day would come. We talked about what to do with the businesses, their money, how they managed everything, who I should trust, and how I should act. At the end of the meeting, he turned and said, "Son, you might not be ready, but the day has come. You must step up and help me in this judicial and political battle that we must face in order to save our family." That day, as a loyal son, I assumed a new role. And, in this way, I entered a new chapter in my life.

Like I said, the majority of criminals are captured due to people like Jorge Salcedo, one of the few men in the world that can say that a life of crime ultimately paid off. This man went through the Colombian judicial system conspiring and committing acts of terrorism. He even speaks of his participation in murders in a book that he published. At the end of it all, he received 1.5 million dollars for turning his boss in, and he has never stepped foot inside of a federal prison.

During the long search for my father and uncle, not a single cop was killed, and in every single raid prior to their capture, not a single shot was fired, which demonstrated that our fight against the government was always judicial, never violent.

CHAPTER 9

On June 15, 1994, the ex-presidential candidate, Andrés Pastrana Arango, received a series of cassettes from the DEA that had conversations that proved that the Cali Cartel had intervened in the presidential campaign in Colombia. One of these tapes led to the discovery of one of the biggest political scandals in Colombia's history, and led to the beginning of the "8,000 Process," which still brings shame to those that participated in it.

Alberto "Loco" Giraldo was a well-known reporter and an expert in public relations with the political lobbyists and the militant conservatives, to which Andrés Pastrana Arango belonged. Giraldo, who met my father after my uncle's capture in Spain in 1984, was a fundamental pillar in bringing my uncle back to Colombia due to his close relationship with the Conservative Party that was in power at that time.

It helps to remember that due to my uncle's capture, my father had been forced to relocate to Bogotá, where he had lived in the Hotel Tequendama. In his suite, he had met with any and all politicians, attorneys, or members of the administration that had ideas or influence over the decision to extradite my uncle to Colombia and not the United States as was originally planned. That's how he met Giraldo. His advice had been instrumental in preventing my uncle's extradition to the US. In fact, his knowledge had been so valuable that my father and uncle had offered him a permanent job in their organization. The two cartel leaders turned a blind eye to the fact that due to his active social life, Giraldo suffered from alcoholism. Models, actresses, the jet set, and parties constituted Giraldo's day-to-day life. This lifestyle led him to make a mistake that would mark the beginning of the end for the Cali Cartel, as it let the American government know that the cartel was one of the biggest corruptors of the Colombian political sphere.

It was a historic moment, perfect for a person like the future liberal candidate, Ernesto Samper Pizano, to offer new, modern ideas to the public. He was a liberal politician that had propelled himself up the ladder not only because of his intellect, but because of his relationship with narcotrafficking: "The problem is a transnational one," he said, "and the relationships are already established." This speech caught the attention of the Cali Cartel, who looked upon him with admiration in this crucial moment, when the international community had opened up their eyes to the world of drug trafficking due to the increased consumption of illicit substances and the exorbitant amounts of money that affected the economies of relatively weak countries in the region. What worried them the most, especially the Americans, was that the underground economy of narcotrafficking would undermine the Plan of the Americas, which had been created by the United States for its allies in this region of the world. In the beginning, that plan had been created to ensure the development of stable democracies in the region, the transformation and prevention of conflicts—all with the end goal of increasing social investment and the replacement of drug farms—but it ended up turning into thoughtless fumigations that hurt the rural workers that depended on the land to earn their livings honestly.

Eduardo Mestre Sarmiento, an important politician that accomplished everything but the presidency, became the perfect bridge to facilitate a conversation with the future liberal candidate, not only because of his knowledge regarding the political sphere, but because of his extraordinary gifts as a negotiator. His close relationship with the candidate allowed him to be aware of his detailed schedule. Mestre was also friends with my father and uncle.

I have fond memories regarding the presence of Mestre in Congress, where he passionately defended every cause he was given. I still remain shocked at how his career came to an end: betrayed by his boss and friend.

Hoping to establish a serious judicial plan and with specific political goals in mind, Mestre set up a meeting in Madrid, where Samper, who was the ambassador to Spain at the time, met with men that represented my father's and uncle's interests.

The goal of the cartel leaders was to be able to reach an agreement where they would be allowed to reintegrate into society and would be allowed to serve their sentence at home, as well as getting lower sentences. The Rodríguez brothers would agree to spearhead a process among drug dealers to reduce the shipment of drugs, which would eventually lead to the end of the business; whoever opposed the plan would have to pay for it judicially. The goals were evident: ending narcotrafficking in Colombia, and setting up a reasonable and decent government. This was the deal struck with the future president of Colombia.

The former deal is remarkably similar to what Álvaro Uribe's government tried to accomplish with the FARC: forgiveness and forgetting, demobilization and reintegration. Sadly, once Ernesto Samper was elected, Giraldo's lack of responsibility would put an end to those good intentions: he made calls that were recorded, without his knowledge, by the government.

The Americans, worried that the future president had "dangerous" friends, had asked the infamous "Gray Men" of the National Police Force to collaborate with them; their mission was to locate the cartel's contact to the political world, track Giraldo's movements, and record his conversations.

This is how they realized that Giraldo communicated with my father and uncle on a daily basis from the apartment where one of his lovers resided.

In the meeting that took place in Madrid, the liberal candidate had agreed to propose a law that would set up a way for drug dealers to submit to justice, if he was elected. The law would be something similar to what Gaviria had done with Escobar and Betancur with M-19. But, due to the scandal caused by the intercepted calls to Giraldo, Congress grew in influence and power and set up a series of laws that would allow them to exploit the government at their will.

The strategy developed by the US was starting to produce positive results. They continued to display how strategically and precisely they managed the distribution of information to manipulate the common people's thoughts. With these tapes in their hands, all they had to do was wait for the perfect moment to detonate this metaphorical bomb and create an avalanche that would end the Cali Cartel and the incoming president.

Santiago Medina, known for being an antiquary and for his glamor, was friends with my uncle Gilberto and his wife due to the fact that they frequented many of the famous clubs in the capital. Due to this relationship, they had negotiated many deals regarding works of art. When he became the treasurer for Samper's campaign, their relationship reignited. The antiquary Medina would travel to Cali whenever he needed to organize the movement of money for the campaign.

The person in charge of optimizing the recollection of money in Cali was a man that worked for my father, who after some time ended up being one of the men affected by Medina when he accepted the charges against him by the government.

Samper, having been elected president, always denied having accepted any money from the drug world, and continues to state this today. The phrase he used, "behind my back," became infamous, and even more famous was the description used by Pedro Rubiano Sanchez, who said that looking at the facts, it would have been as if an elephant had entered a person's home and no one noticed.

Unfortunately and inexplicably, at some point my father and uncle—both men with extensive experience dealing with intelligence-gathering systems—took these calls from Giraldo. In these phone calls, Giraldo described the strategies used by the campaign in detail, the financial needs that they had, and the difficulties posed by the opposing campaign, for Pastrana, that was gaining more and more support by the day. Eventually, they even considered the possibility of contributing funds to both campaigns.

The comments made by Giraldo were unnecessary, seeing as my father and uncle had put a plane and the corresponding staff at his disposal so that he could fly to Cali and meet with them whenever necessary.

That plane was used to transport Giraldo, Ovejo—a man that worked with my father—and the antiquary Medina, who were all in charge of collecting money from Cali and making sure it was used by the campaign in whatever city it was needed to accomplish the goal of winning the first round.

Seeing as the number of votes necessary to win on the first round was not achieved by any candidate, as instructed by the Constitution, a second round was needed. The liberal candidate, worried about the strain that a second round would place on his campaign, constantly sent requests and reminders of his promise to Cali.

My father and uncle, upon receiving those reaffirming words from Samper, made great efforts to collect the amount of money that was needed to propel the campaign. It is worth mentioning that the political project of submission that they were attempting to establish by financing the campaign could have been the start of the end of a problem that did not only affect my father and uncle. The project had good intentions and the intellect and capabilities of the president elect only made it that much more probable and worth defending. The objective was to end the business of drug trafficking; hypothetically, the business would falter if they controlled the shipment of drugs from Colombia and dealers were forced to give up their routes.

It was a bad idea in the eyes of those that planned to continue on indirectly getting rich through the business, and awful in the eyes of those that held their personal interests on top of anything that implicated a possible negotiation.

Andrés Pastrana Arango became the bastion of morality: with his usual excess of make-up and theatrics, he turned to the media demanding that President Ernesto Samper Pizano step down due to the presence of dirty money in his campaign. In the first round, the Cali Cartel provided a sum equivalent to 4 million dollars; in the second round, they donated 6 million dollars more. A donation that did not exactly aim to elect a president, but to reach an agreement with government so that they could end one of the biggest problems that Colombian society was facing.

From this moment on, speculation and the "8,000 Process" spearheaded by Alfonso Valdivieso Sarmiento became the topic of conversation in the government and in society for over a decade. The "8,000 Process" had so much influence that Valdivieso even aimed to become president due to the influence he won over it. His bid for presidency was harshly questioned when he opposed the contribution and involvement of a certain faction of the Colombian government that had always tried to appear as pure and incorruptible.

The district attorney's office, working closely with the United States' Consulate, developed a simple strategy: get Samper to step down. To do this, they put pressure on Medina and the other members that formed part of the campaign's administration. His vice president, Humberto de la Calle, whom the US officials viewed in a favorable light, could lead the judiciary. Plus, de la Calle was close to the ex-president Gaviria, his natural leader, and who, from the OEA, could tell him exactly what targets to hit in order to continue with the Plan of the Americas.

Political interests always outweigh the judicial ones, according to a maxim by the United States. Samper did not step down, which meant that Medina, the campaign's treasurer, and Fernando Botero Zea, who was the campaign's secretary, would both go to prison. Colombia: a country where the secretary and treasurer of a campaign end up in jail but the president elect is absolved.

Samper refused to step down, an act that forced the US to abandon their current strategy. Instead, they decided to make him their ally and to let him know exactly what his political agenda was to be during his tenure. In doing this, they let not only the country but the entire world know that Samper had nothing to do with anyone related to the drug-trafficking world.

Effectively, during Samper's presidency, laws regarding forfeiture that allowed the government to keep any property that had been tainted with drug money were passed. Money laundering was categorized as an automatic federal offence. The stigma around dirty money became so great that any person could be accused of this, even those that had taken property in their names for criminals.

During his tenure, there was constant communication between the president and my father and uncle. The good president constantly blackmailed them by threatening their well-being in certain prisons and with their permanence in the country, telling them that if they ever said anything in regards to their monetary contributions, he would extradite them immediately. As a result, my father and uncle never spoke about this.

CHAPTER 10

After my father and uncle were both captured, I had to take the reins of the organization, a responsibility that would change my life forever. Before this, I navigated my world around their mandates and their parameters, building a life like everyone else's, far away from the criminal world, and building a career as a lawyer and businessman, which had been their dream for all of us.

But, due to the unfortunate circumstances we were in, someone had to step up and take care of our family—their well-being was the reason and the motivation behind my decision to embark down a path from which I would not be able to return, and one that would almost end my life. Having searched for respect and approval from my father during my entire life, this was the perfect opportunity to show him what I was made of, that I shared his DNA and was just as capable.

Unknowingly, I was entering a fight that I could not win. The US agencies had their eyes set on Colombia, not only because they wanted to end drug trafficking there, but because they wanted more influence over the gateway to South America, and the influx of revenue from illicit businesses was providing a push in their economies which would make them less dependent on Uncle Sam. They did not want this influx of cash to generate more problems than the ones they already had in different areas in the world.

Their plan had three objectives, and to attain them, they negotiated with their Colombian footmen. To achieve the first, ending the drug-trafficking business, they took advantage of the scandal surrounding Samper, who was stained from the revelation that his campaign had accepted dirty money from the Cali Cartel, and forced him to introduce and attain laws that allowed for the forfeiture of property and that legalized extradition of nationals. The other two objectives were the "Plan Colombia": a bilateral agreement between the US and Colombia that was signed in 1999, with the goal of creating a revitalization of the social and economic conditions in the country, ending the armed conflict, creating a strategy to end drug trafficking, and to create free trade agreements, which, today, are actually directly responsible for bankrupting many areas of the Colombian economy.

I began gaining recognition in this context, but, fundamentally, I got it within the scheme needed by my father to coordinate his defense and to stop any legal processes in Congress during the reign of President Ernesto Samper.

During this critical period, I started exhibiting drastic changes in my personality. I discovered that power is a narcotic that slowly clouds your conscience, that makes you believe that the ends justify the means, and that makes you forget the values instilled in you at home all so that you can achieve the result that you want.

I went through a great metamorphosis: I went from being a person like any other to being a type of superhuman that believed he could do anything, taking on assignments and making promises to my father that any person in their right mind would have never agreed to. Like I said, I needed his recognition, and he needed someone that was willing to risk it all in this judicial war against the American empire.

One of the first missions that I was given by him was to look for a way to negotiate with the government and to clarify their position on the promises made to them in Spain regarding some kind of law that would allow them to turn themselves and their businesses in and that would give them lower sentences. Plus, they wanted me to start working on stopping the law that was being developed in Congress in relation to illegal enrichment. This law was perilous to my family's judicial stability and to the same congressmen that had been involved in the "8,000 Process."

I spoke to a political contact in Cartago known as "El Gordo," who had been a family friend of the Sampers for many years, and who had carried out various tasks for the cartel before. In the meeting that we had, which took place in Bogotá, I expressed our need for a way to approach the government to clear up our situation. I heard nothing from him for about two months.

In 1995, at the end of November, I received a call from El Gordo. He told me that he had an important message from the government and that my presence was needed as soon as possible in Bogotá. His friend, Fernando Botero Zea, was about to tell the truth regarding the financing for the 1994 presidential campaign, where the Cali Cartel had invested about 10 million dollars. The current government's minister wanted to schedule a meeting in Cantón Norte, a military base in the north of Bogotá where the ex-minister Botero was detained due to his involvement in the narco-cassettes. They wanted to ease his worries, telling him that what we had discussed was still going to happen, and that we were willing to use whatever resources were necessary to stop the upcoming laws about forfeiture of assets and illicit enrichment. If Congress passed this law and it individualized drug trafficking and subversion as a crime, he was going to be the first person sentenced.

A messenger that worked for Fernando Botero Zea picked me up at a superstore in El Chico, a neighborhood in Bogotá. I was accompanied by Congressman Chavarriaga, who supposedly opposed the passing of these laws due to ideological differences— he believed these laws were regressive—but his real interest was much more material than that. He knew that these laws could be used against them—the congressmen and the senators—if they were passed, which they were.

We made our way into the Canton at around midnight, evading any kind of security checkpoint. Ex-minister Botero and the current minister were waiting for us in the officers' lounge. In this meeting, and after discussing the current state of the country, Botero spoke firmly; he was not willing to go to prison over illicit enrichment charges, and it shocked him that this crime was about to be individualized in Congress.

The government minister tried to calm him down, assuring him that the president would do whatever was in his power to make sure that did not happen. He also said that the reason he had been sent there was to reaffirm all of this in the president's good name. I informed the ex-minister of the actions we had been taking in Congress with the help of Congressman Chavarriaga and others. I tried to get him to believe in the actions that were being taken and asked him to be sensible. I explained that it was in everyone's best interests to get this situation under control due to the instability that this would bring to Colombia, and that we had to stop extradition of nationals because it would affect not only my father and uncle, but him as well.

The debates that took place in Congress were difficult and, in the end, we lost them because the media was being controlled by the ambassador to the US, Myles Frechette, and he used them to frighten senators and representatives into submission.

Fernando Botero Zea, having been betrayed by his former boss and after being charged with illicit enrichment, contacted me in order to set up another meeting in the military base he was in. We met on Friday, January 19, 1996, when night fell. He informed me that he was going to tell the truth regarding this embarrassing moment in Colombia's history. He was going to do this and did not care how that would affect him or us. He knew that no matter what happened, his career as a politician was already over.

The news cycle on Monday, January 22, 1996, opened up with a scandalous headline: "Botero spills all." When asked whether or not the current president was aware that his campaign had been accepting money from drug traffickers, the ex-minister said, "Yes, the president knew about the drug money that was being invested into his campaign."

That night, the army and the air force put on a spectacle in the capital. Samper was clear: "I am here, and I am staying!" He was confident in this because he was being backed by the Americans, to whom he had recently promised the end of drug trafficking, showing his true treasonous and Machiavellian nature, and willing to betray everyone that had helped him get to where he was.

During this time, and before my assassination attempt, our family lived through many other tumultuous moments. I had taken on the lead role for our family in the world of politics and corruption, buying our way out of any kind of problem, constantly putting my life at risk. I was destined for prison or death. I took on massive battles like the one with Botero or setting up meetings with the big players of the drug world in order to keep my family standing on solid ground. The most dangerous of these was a meeting I had with Carlos Castaño and the leaders of the North Valley Cartel in Córdoba.

I can't say that I did not enjoy what I was doing. I lived in a state of trance produced by the constant release of adrenaline that constantly fed my ego on a hopeless quest for power and recognition. I forgot about the most important things in life, like my wife Maria and my beautiful daughter.

While I went through this period, I began having serious problems in my marital life. Maria did not approve of the way I was handling things. Her sixth sense, which was and still is superior to my impulses, told her that this would not end well. For this reason, she constantly reminded me of how disappointed she was in the person that I was becoming. The normal, loving man that she had fallen in love with in college was completely lost in this new beastly being that had lost its way. Her comments annoyed me. When you're living outside of reality, you only hear what you want to. Without worrying about the consequences, I almost ended my marriage, believing that it was nothing compared to the power that I, in my mind, was accumulating. I ignored the fact that I was swimming in dangerous waters because I was too enamored with my own ego.

This was around the time when I met a beautiful woman with blue eyes that were as deep as the ocean. She helped me; I found comfort and refuge in her arms at a time when I felt completely alone. Her words, always positive, made these difficult times a little easier. But this was a love that could not be, due to the significant age difference between us; I think she has been the only woman that might have had a chance in separating me from my family. To this day, I remember Paulina fondly.

In May 1996, everything became even more complicated after I was shot and almost killed by the North Valley Cartel. We were almost wiped out by that group of criminals, who had no values or morals. This attempt on my life changed everything for me. I understood that there are things in life that are worth a lot more than power or recognition. Unfortunately, I did not see this before, and I learned a tough lesson: every time I look at myself in the mirror and catch a glimpse of my scars, I am reminded of the physical pain I felt and the emotional pain that will never subside over the loss of my friends.

Only the dedication and love that I received from my wife at this critical time, surrounded by fear, gave me the strength that I needed to recover and to change my life. This was how I was able to keep my home, understanding that, at the end of the day, the only thing that we have left is the love and support of the people that stand by our side.

During fifteen months, I had lived a life clouded by delusion, believing that I could touch the sky and accomplish the impossible: taking unnecessary risks, corrupting wills and consciences, and trying to win a war that had been lost from the start. We had been crazy to think that we could take on a giant like the United States of America.

In June 1996, I made the decision, with my wife's support, to leave all of this craziness behind and flee to Argentina. As soon as we had prepared everything, we learned that I had been formally accused by a court in Florida as part of a case called "Piedra Angular" against the Cali Cartel. This case was being led by Special Agent Edward Kacerosky. According to the United States, I was the new leader of the Cali Cartel.

Due to this news, I lived one of the worst moments of my life. I wanted to flee, but I could not put a foot outside of Colombian territory; I had an international arrest warrant issued by Interpol called a Red Notice—if I left the country, I would be arrested immediately and handed over to the North American authorities.

During the time that I spent recuperating from the attempt on my life, we were trying to achieve a ceasefire agreement between the Cali Cartel and the North Valley Cartel. Because of the attempt on my life, there was increased tension between the two cartels, but, fortunately, I survived and was able to clear up the misunderstandings caused by Don Efra—who had made them up in order to eliminate all competition and become the number one drug dealer. According to him, my father and uncle were their biggest obstacle and were behind every anonymous tip that the attorney's office received.

There were many meetings in La Picota, the prison where my father and uncle were being kept, between them and Orlando Henao in order to reach an agreement. In one of these meetings, my father explained that the best chance any of them stood was to face the laws regarding forfeiture and illicit enrichment together. Henao agreed. The North Valley Cartel agreed to gather money from anyone involved in the business, and we agreed to barter a deal.

Who was to be in charge of dealing with politicians? The leaders of the North Valley Cartel insisted that I should be the one to do this. At first, my father refused, but, due to their insistence, he was forced to accept, which was when I was called to partake in one of the meetings in La Picota. My uncle began to explain what was at risk if I refused this task: our family's financial stability and his honor, as he had given his word to the other bosses.

In the beginning, I refused. I felt weak, physically and mentally. I didn't think that I could deliver what they wanted if I was not at my best. And, I felt uneasy at the thought of working with men that had recently tried to have me killed. My father told me to think about it. If I showed these men any sign of resentment against them, I would be putting my life and the lives of those I cared about at risk … I had to be smart, he said. He assured me that there would come a time for us to seek revenge on them for what they had done.

After much thought, I decided that my father was right. I was caught in a net with no foreseeable way out—a good metaphor for what my life had turned into at that moment. I accepted my role spearheading this fight, which I knew could not be won, out of loyalty and respect for my father.

In the middle of the war that we were in with the Congress of the Republic to stop these laws that were harmful to all drug traffickers, I met up with Fabio Ochoa Jr., the youngest member of the Ochoa clan, in the lobby of the Hotel Tequendama in Bogotá. I tried to explain what was at risk, telling him that it was not just my family that was to be affected by this, that they were coming for all of us.

I don't think Fabio understood my explanation regarding the details and consequences of this law. He did not understand the repercussions that it would have. Like many other figures in narco-trafficking, he believed that these were laws fabricated with the sole purpose of ending the Cali Cartel and that they would not affect anyone else. Later, he and the others would feel the pain that we had in their own flesh due to the damaging effects of this law and the resolve of the American government to hit drug organizations where it hurt them the most: their pockets. Obviously, they knew that if they took away our funds, we would not be able to put up a good fight in the courts or in Congress.

Fabio offered $50,000. I told him that I would speak with my father about this and get back to him. I knew that this sum was too small and that my father would be offended by this insignificant offer.

When it came time for this law to be approved, Chavarriaga and I reached a conclusion: there were only two ways to win the debate in the Chamber of Representatives. One was to speak with the Minister of the Government, who was a skilled orator with a lot of influence—he always beat us if he was on the opposing side—to convince him to not show up that day. The other was to call in a favor with an Afro-Colombian congressman from El Choco, to whom we gave $100,000 to oppose the bill, which he did.

In the meeting we scheduled with the Minister of the Government, we were able to convince him to be absent on the day of the debate. I pleaded my case by reminding him that he came from a liberal background and explaining that this law was retroactive. It was a law meant to punish, even though they wanted to make it seem that it was for administrative purposes. In the end, to make sure that we accomplished our goals, I brought up our support in keeping the president's image clean.

The Minister of the Government traveled to Barrancabermeja the day of the vote so he could be present at an event they were throwing in his native town in his honor. That same night, every member of the press asked the same thing, "Where was the Minister of the Government?"

We had attained victory in this battle against the empire and its lackeys in the Colombian senate.

We put up a good fight in the war for our economic future and the ones of our families. We had tied the vote in the Chamber of Representatives, which led to a vote in the Senate, where we lost. This defeat meant that we would need to double our efforts, and it meant that the promises I had made to my family and to the North Valley Cartel, which had abandoned us in the middle of the fight, were in danger.

When the results between the representatives and the Senate do not agree with one another, they construct a committee in charge of bridging the gap and coming up with a result. They chose fifteen honorable members of parliament, most of whom were in our pockets, to make up the committee. The leaders of the North Valley Cartel did not understand what was happening, and they refused to give us the amount of money that was needed.

We had to prove to these members of parliament that we were liquid, but we were unable to do so. We lost the vote because the government, pressured by the media and the Americans, gave all of the members of the committee an incentive when we couldn't. The result was fourteen to one, and the law passed. That was the moment we lost our economic stability and a great part of the judicial battle.

Sad and defeated, in a hotel in Bogotá, I realized that there was nothing more we could do. Our luck had run out, and the upcoming judicial battle was basically won by the American government and the top 1% of Colombian society, who also wanted us out. One of my friends, who was part of M-19, had been correct: we shouldn't have wasted any more money and time on laws and political processes.

Threatened from all angles, our only hope was to resort to political acts or acts of violence. The way that we had been brought up had always led us to choose the judicial way, which is why we were ultimately defeated; but that was our philosophy, our way of life, and we would not betray that.

CHAPTER 11

Don Chepe, or simply Chepe to his family and friends, was the person that first introduced my uncle and father to the world of drug trafficking. Aside from this business, they were united by a bond forged through years of friendship and loyalty. There were many ups and downs in this friendship, like when Chepe fled La Picota with my father's blessing.

Chepe had been the typical bohemian man from the Sixties. Aside from his warmth, his way of always bringing up the mood in a room, and his spontaneity, he was an extremely loyal friend and an unforgiving enemy. Because of his personality, even Hélmer "Pacho" Herrera held him in high regards. My uncle Gilberto, on the other hand, always looked at him with suspicion: Chepe always made decisions without consulting him, so my uncle thought he was a loose cannon that could damage the rest of the group.

He liked to dress informally and to eat at the finest places. On a day like any other, as he ate at a restaurant called Carbon de Palo in Bogotá, and after a long day of gathering intelligence—dealing with informants, monetary rewards, etc.—he was captured and jailed in the same place as his old partners.

My uncle and father were kept in the maximum-security wing, Pavillion B, of La Picota. When Chepe arrived there, the only one out of the four original leaders of the cartel was Pacho Herrera.

During my many visits to La Picota, I came to realize that Chepe was an awful prisoner. He constantly complained about what he believed was not only a dirty trick of fate but a betrayal by the ruling class in Colombia. The bourgeoisie had accepted them for more than twenty years and had participated in multiple business ventures with the "dons of Cali," recognizing them as serious businessmen who respected the institutions, but they were now turning their backs on them.

Chepe's slogan was simple: as long as he lived, he would never give up his way of life. He made sure to live by this slogan, even while he was in prison. He believed that in order to maintain the control and the respect that they wanted, not only from other criminals but from the State itself, they could not give up their status or their money. My uncle and father, on the other hand, wanted to distance themselves from the business, naively believing that the North American authorities would forgive their past mistakes; they really believed that they could achieve the impossible: intervene with the policies being placed on the State by Washington, maintaining some kind of protagonism that would, in the end, be their downfall.

Ernesto Samper Pizano, having been elected president, had declared himself an enemy of drug trafficking due to the scandal surrounding the "8,000 Process," and was working on a series of projects in Congress that would make our lives miserable. Chepe believed that, sooner or later, they would reinstate extradition and that they, as former bosses of the Cali Cartel, would be the first to go.

Time would end up proving him right, and today my father and uncle find themselves incarcerated in the United States with no way to return.

When he was arrested, Chepe immediately delegated the handling of numerous tasks. The power and respect that he possessed while he was free began to diminish when he was in jail. This was a result not only of being imprisoned, but also of the ambition of those who were not in jail and saw this as an opportunity to grow in the business.

In Cali, there was a well-known character in the underground world of drugs and crime known as Capulina, a hired assassin that had gotten rich due to drug trafficking and who reveled in partying and living in luxury. In Jamundí, a municipality just six miles from the south of Cali, a conflict occurred between Capulina and a close relative of "El Sejo," Chepe's deputy. Capulina later found out that the man with whom he had exchanged rough words and threats was the relative of Chepe's most-trusted accomplice. Capulina, scared, turned to Orlando Henao and told him his skewed side of the story, asking him to intervene on his behalf in front of my father and uncle so that they could stop Chepe's orders to kill him. Orlando Henao, El Sejo, and Capulina met with my father, my uncle, and Chepe in the Picota maximum security wing, Pavilion B. After having lunch, they recounted what had gone down in Jamundí. Capulina, knowing that he had made a mistake, asked for forgiveness and Chepe accepted this, but El Sejo could not accept this and still gave orders to murder Capulina. This created tensions between the two cartels, but Chepe, sure of who he was and of his power, backed up "El Sejo." A grave mistake. The leaders of the North Valley Cartel, to whom Capulina had asked for help as a member of their organization, saw these actions as acts of defiance, and, in this way, a conflict ensued that led not only to Capulina's murder, but that would place us in an uncomfortable position for a long time.

During that time and before his death due to a heart attack, the man that was responsible for resolving conflicts between the two cartels was Ivan Urdinola Grajales. He was imprisoned with my father and uncle, and he always tried to lessen the effects of any situation that could affect everyone's peace of mind. After he was captured, my father and uncle considered distancing themselves from all illegal activities in the hope of becoming some sort of "legal bandits," as I once referred to them.

Every choice had to be deeply evaluated, analyzing every single consequence that could occur; and, if it was true that they had won a lot of power in the war with Escobar, it was also true that, in that moment, they were not only being persecuted by the United States and Colombia, but also that the businesses and the family were suffering due to the choices they had made as leaders, putting all of our futures at risk in the hands of their many enemies. For this reason, my uncle never agreed with the way Chepe handled himself, and constantly reproached him for his mistake with Capulina until he fled the prison. He had given his word, and instead of murdering him, he could have utilized the connection they had with Ivan Urdinola to prevent future aggressions. Nobody believed him when he claimed that "El Sejo" had made the decision by himself.

In the Santa Librada School of Cali, my father had always distinguished himself as being an expert in calligraphy and in drawing, passions he still cultivates and that he chose to work on when he became a prisoner. With the help of a college student that was fulfilling some requisite by volunteering at La Picota, my father managed to reconstruct the entire prison by scale, not only the outside but the cells, the hallways, the masonry, all electronic security measures; he believed that he might eventually have to escape from the prison, and these drawings were his way out of extradition. He carelessly shared this project with Chepe, who, without his knowledge, made a copy of them and used them to plan his own escape.

The Colombian justice system had created the concept of "faceless judges," a dark and inquisition-like practice that brings us great shame to this day. These men used to be brought into the maximum-security pavilion of La Picota in armor-plated vehicles with tinted windows, in order to keep them "faceless," incorruptible. Nobody, not even the INPEC officers who were in charge of guarding the prisons, could see their faces; they were only allowed to verify their identity as judges. There were countless disciplinary processes that were taken against INPEC guards that had violated the identity of the faceless prosecutors and judges while opening the doors to these vehicles. It wasn't hard to see the ease with which one could access these men and replace them with anyone, which was what Chepe planned to do. He met with "El Sejo" and told him his plan: they would follow the vehicles that came from the DA's office into the maximum-security pavilion and would record their daily routine. The next step was to get a vehicle that was identical to the ones used by the DAs and, when it was ready, to carry out the escape plan. It was scheduled for the first week of the month, the week when most errors occurred in their highly synchronized routine.

The vehicle that Chepe's men had created in resemblance to the armor-plated vehicles made it inside La Picota undetected: supposedly, there was a faceless judge inside of it. In reality, the men that traveled in it were "El Sejo" and his assistant. Carefully instructed by Chepe, these two men carried with them copies of the drawings created by my father and the tools necessary to carry out their plan.

It was around 2 p.m. on February 11, 1996, and the usual lunch with lawyers, family, and friends was coming to an end. Chepe went up to the table where my father and uncle were seated, and he said goodbye to them, telling them that he was leaving, that he had been called by a guard because his presence was requested by a faceless judge in one of the cubicles. His friends laughed at his words; it was the last time they saw him alive.

With Chepe inside of the cubicle, his men began to take it apart with the tools that had been smuggled in the "cloned" vehicle. Chepe squeezed himself through the tinted crystal. Once they had reinstalled the glass, they left the prison under the protection offered to them by the guise of a "faceless" judge.

At four o'clock, the captain that was in charge of getting a headcount of the prisoners in the pavilion grew pale as he realized that they could not find José Santacruz Londoño anywhere. He asked the other men, who informed him that he had been called to a cubicle by a faceless judge around two o'clock. The captain hurried to the cubicles; after realizing that no one was inside, he gave the alert that José Santacruz Londoño had fled. The first measure they took was to lock down all of the prisoners under strict rules, including my father and uncle, who were going through difficult times as they feared extradition.

The National Police took over the pavilion, and every single INPEC officer was discharged and investigated.

After hiding for eight days in Bogotá, Chepe traveled to

Medellín, with the intention of smoothing things over with the North Valley Cartel, which had made it its mission to end what remained of the Cali Cartel. To do this, he decided to meet with one of Escobar's old allies that had a relationship with the cartel's bosses because they had started to finance his war against the guerrillas. To discuss matters, Carlos Castaño suggested a meeting, one which required the presence of both Chepe and Pacho Herrera, in a house near Las Palmas in Medellín.

Pacho always doubted Castaño's loyalty; he thought he was nothing more than a mercenary. According to him, Fidel Castaño, founder of the AUC, who had been an ally to the Cali Cartel during the war with Pablo, had been his friend and had been killed at the hands of his brother Carlos, leaving Carlos as the sole leader of the AUC. Luckily, Pacho decided to not attend the meeting, sending in his place a trusted ally and changing his hiding place as he awaited news.

When he got to the meeting, Chepe found that Castaño was in the presence of around twenty heavily armed men, something unusual for a meeting of this kind. When he realized that Orlando Henao and Efrain Antonio "Don Efra" Hernández were also there, he realized that Carlos Castaño, his friend, had betrayed him.

Chepe and Pacho Herrera's envoy were tortured in order to get any information on Pacho's location. This plan had been agreed to by Colonel Danilo González so that they could give the National Police a positive result with the death and capture of Chepe and Pacho, but they were only able to get Chepe.

In an absurd show full of theatrics, where they claimed they had listened to the testimony of a man, the National Police informed the public that José Santacruz Londoño had been neutralized. The National Police's killer bullets that ended Chepe's life could not be linked back to them. This case was never investigated due to the fact that this fell perfectly into the crazed mission by the National Police to end drug trafficking at whatever cost.

When Chepe died, our enemies were brought to light, which

brought on many difficulties for my entire family. Any kind of testimony, true or not, was exploited by the North Valley Cartel to excuse exterminating us. What friends my father had left told him that they needed to have a meeting where a representative of the Rodríguez family was present and willing to clear up the many things the opposing cartel was accusing us of. This meeting was scheduled midway through March 1996, in the presence of Carlos Castaño and his new-found allies. The trip to Montería required an overnight stay in Bogotá; the only flight that went directly to that city was always scheduled for departure from the capital at 7.30 a.m.

Having scheduled everything, I noticed that Don Efra was on my same flight. He politely acknowledged me. This event was quickly overlooked, but would later carry great significance. Once in Montería, my cousin Humberto and I booked a room in a hotel located in the city's main plaza. After a couple of hours, we were picked up by a man that looked like he was in the military, who skillfully drove through the rural streets. The trip to the designated location lasted about an hour and a half.

It was a nice country home with two buildings and a little kiosk that was heavily guarded by men who wore AUC armbands. These men blindly followed the directions of their leader, Carlos Castaño, who had organized this meeting and that, ultimately, would decide the results.

Castaño welcomed us and asked us to proceed to the kiosk. He was surrounded by at least twenty men, the most important figures in drug trafficking, led by Orlando Henao and Don Efra. Castaño began to give a speech justifying Chepe's murder; he repeatedly stated that Chepe, as well as the Rodríguez family, were allies to the guerrillas. He stated that this was reason enough to execute him.

After, Don Efra spoke. He claimed that my father and uncle were rats that constantly provided the DA's office with information on them related to drug trafficking. This man easily forgot the countless amounts of injured men and the widows that he had left behind due to his psychopathic ego. Then, Orlando Henao said he agreed with Don Efra and confidently repeated what he was sure was a fact: the supposed testimonies.

After their interventions, I refuted the arguments they had made and appealed to their sense of logic; I asked them to not try to cover the sun with a single finger and to understand that their sole business was drug trafficking, and it made no sense for them to blame all of their woes on a single person or group. I reminded them of the countless number of times that my uncle and father had extended entrepreneurial solidarity, if you can call it that. They had informed them of people within their own organizations that were informing on them. I also reminded Carlos Castaño that on various occasions he had traveled to Cali with the sole purpose of meeting with my father and uncle during the war with Escobar, and that he had no proof or any reason at all to suspect that they were trying to hand him over to the guerrillas.

Once I had stated my position, Carlos Castaño took the lead in speaking amongst men who were deadly silent. He said that from now on, my cousin and I were to be responsible for whatever act of treason that could be proven and that would affect, directly or indirectly, the businesses of the North Valley Cartel.

It was obvious that there was no going back. The stage was set. We were enemies. The death of Chepe and Don Efra's malicious intent were the fuel that would feed the fire that was coming.

Chepe's memory will remain forever ingrained in the hearts of his family and his friends. He had been a visionary that knew what had to be done and did it. In the end, he is the freest one of them all; he preferred a tombstone in Colombia than a jail cell in the United States.

My father and uncle dreamed of turning their fortune legit through the judicial and political systems. They were only willing to pay small sentences from home, and wanted to keep working in their businesses and corporations until retirement like any founder of any business.

But on their way to this goal, they made too many mistakes.

They did not take the opportunity that they had to turn themselves in and negotiate. They could have done the same amount of time as the Ochoa family, who, in my opinion, were able to truly navigate their chessboard as they stuck to a discreet lifestyle. All of them were able to get their lives back, except Fabio, who continued to surround himself with drug traffickers and ended up being extradited to the United States.

Not two months had passed since the infamous meeting in Montería when, on a particularly warm day—Friday, May 24, 1996—I woke up with every intention to visit a church in Buga, a municipality located about an hour from the north of Cali. The figure of Christ that is found there is venerated by the Catholic Community as "miraculous." The day before, Thursday, May 23, Edgar "Mono" Veloza had been killed. He was an ex-military lieutenant that had worked with my uncle as head of security during the war with Escobar.

Mono Veloza's murder had been the trigger for my assassination attempt the following day, and was the result of the misinterpretation of words by Guillermo Villa Alzate, who had been my father's trusted attorney. Villa Alzate had been kidnapped and taken to Orlando Henao and Don Efra. They wanted him to tell them who had been behind two anonymous tips delivered to the DA's office, in which they had denounced their drug- trafficking and money-laundering activities. They claimed that these had been written and sent by my father and uncle. Villa Alzate assured them that he had no knowledge of these anonymous tips, which he claimed were unimportant, but he also assured them that he did know of other times when my father had sent in tips. With no further explanations needed, the new bosses of the drug-trafficking world found the perfect excuse to begin hunting us down.

What Villa Alzate had really been referring to was a situation that occurred with Carlos Alfonso Velásquez, when he was spearheading the Search Bloc in Cali. He had persecuted my father and uncle tirelessly. This ex-colonel had been seduced by a woman that had been hired by my father and had been recorded in the middle of a sexual act, which led to his firing. The truth behind what Villa Alzate had tried to explain was only brought to light after the assassination attempts that occurred on May 23 and 24 in 1996.

CHAPTER 12

When I woke up from my surgery, after the assassination attempt where I had been shot eight times, the first thing I remember is seeing my wife's face next to me. As soon as I opened my eyes, I asked her about Fernando Parra, and, with a trembling voice, she told me that he had died on the table a couple of hours ago.

I was praying for the salvation of Fernando's soul when Maria handed me her phone. My father was on the other end of the line, and he wanted to know how I was feeling and exactly how everything had gone down; I gave him evasive answers. I told him that what mattered was that I was alive, and that I thought it was prudent to think of nothing else but the safety and peace of mind of my family. He continued to question me about the men, but I knew that our conversation was being monitored by the authorities and our enemies, who had started coming to light, so I asked him to be prudent. The two months that followed during my recovery were spent in the hospital and at home. These were months filled with anxiety, not just due to the increased security detail around us but because of the moments we found ourselves in.

After my father and uncle were arrested, a strong movement began deep inside Cali and within the growing North Valley Cartel. Many meetings were held in various cities all around the country and even in La Picota, the prison in Bogotá. These meetings were usually between representatives of both sides, including Orlando Henao, who repeatedly tried to put out the fires caused by the animosity felt by Efrain Hernández, Don Efra, and Wilber Alirio Varela, alias "Jabon."

Orlando Henao and Don Efra were now the biggest players in drug trafficking. They controlled the business and the National

Police due to their friend Colonel Danilo González; plus, they had the number one leader of the AUC, Carlos Castaño, in their pocket. With this much power, I never understood why these two men wasted so much of their time and effort on continually trying to prove who was in charge. I always tried to assure them of this reality in the various meetings I was forced to attend in order to put many of their made-up rumors against my father and uncle to rest. Time would later punish them twofold for all their wrong-doings, proving once again that the divine judgment is superior to that of men.

Don Efra was murdered in his office, which was located in an exclusive sector in Bogotá, by Cifuentes, one of his closest allies, whom he constantly bullied, physically and mentally. The killer, taking advantage of the current state of things and knowing the hate that his former boss felt toward the Rodríguez family, tried to blame the murder on us. The killer had been called to Don Efra's office in order to discuss a large sum of money that he had taken and had no way of repaying. Taking advantage of the familiarity he had with Don Efra's secretary, he asked to use the bathroom, where he hid a Colt 45. When he showed up to the meeting that he had been called to in order to satisfy all accounts, he found that Don Efra was waiting for him in the company of his accountant and another one of his men. He waited for the secretary to leave for lunch and, making sure that there was no one else present, asked to use the bathroom. He returned to the meeting with the gun in his hand and shot them all at point-blank range; later, he left the office as if nothing had happened.

The killer, without knowing that Herman, the other man that had been there in the meeting, had survived, took a call from Orlando Henao, who wanted to know what had occurred. The culprit assured him that the Rodríguez family was behind the murder. Orlando Henao set up a meeting with him and killed him, having heard directly from Herman's mouth what had actually happened.

When Don Efra died, Orlando Henao understood that his

real enemies were not my father and uncle, that the real enemy of all drug traffickers was the United States and, logically, its allies in the Colombian government.

After my assassination attempt, I had to take certain responsibilities in my father's name. For this reason, I met with Orlando Henao; it was not easy being face to face with the man that had caused me so much pain, but I learned how to act in order to survive that dark period in my life. Orlando assured me that he was glad to see that I was OK and used the presence of Nicol Parra, who was the head of security for my father, as an excuse for what had gone down. He concluded that my friends and I had been collateral damage and were in the wrong place at the wrong time.

Sadly, the damage was done. The headlines around the world said things like, "Six men killed and one injured, the son and heir of the Cali Cartel." The police, the district attorney's office, and the agencies from the United States needed a new boss, someone to pin everything on, and who better than the son of Miguel Rodríguez, "the new leader of the Cali Cartel."

The need for power and the constant warring over the drug business would give way to another war, in which both Pacho Herrera and Orlando Henao would lose their lives, the latter falling victim to Pacho Herrera's paraplegic brother, who emptied his revolver on Henao's body in a prison cell.

In these murders they also tried to blame my father and uncle due to their proximity to Pacho Herrera, and I was forced to attend yet another mediation to prevent the extermination of my family. Luckily, I was backed by reliable men like Hernando "Rasguno" Gomez, Gabriel Puerta, and Ivan Urdinola. These men, who had their heads on straight, explained who had been responsible for each of these murders and how they had been done—marking a time period when I had not only neutralized our natural enemy, the DA's office, but also the band of Talibans that were constantly coming up with excuses to end our lives.

Many of these men that claimed to be the new bosses of the

drug-trafficking world firmly believed that my father and uncle were on their knees, but this was not the case: they were just waiting for the perfect opportunity to get revenge on those who had repeatedly hurt us. Luckily for me, the proverb that says "I will sit on my balcony and watch as my enemies' coffins pass below me" has proven to be true; I have seen them all. We never moved a single finger to end their lives; their assassination attempt against my life turned into a curse against them for having ended the lives of multiple innocent men.

I attended all the meetings I had to in order to clear our names, denying the comments and ill-intentioned lies crafted by Jabon. He was a sinister man that never forgave my uncle for giving an order to end his life, when he failed to uphold a promise he had made when he killed a close ally of the Cali Cartel in the war with Medellín. My uncle had been talked out of this decision by Orlando Henao and had pardoned his life, but men like him never forget and are never grateful; on the other hand, he continuously tried to concoct rumors to get us killed. Only the loyalty of a friend like Rasguno was able to save us.

But there was another problem. My assassination attempt, mixed with my intervention in Congress, the affinity that politicians had during the many discussions regarding the new laws, and the knowledge I had as a jurist and as an attorney, had made me the perfect target for the United States, that now did not intend to solely extradite my father and uncle, but rather our entire family.

When I learned of what was going on, I hopelessly tried to remain under the radar, but my ego and my obsession with the wrong things—power, money, recognition—had already led me down a dark path, one in which the less horrible thing would be prison, because, thanks to a miracle, I was able to survive the murderous bullets fired by the North Valley Cartel; a life that corroborates the simple fact that a life of crime can only lead you to two places: a tomb or a cell.

After almost losing my life, I dedicated myself to my businesses and to soccer, and I started practicing law again, taking advantage of the many connections I had made in the past years. I saw my efforts rewarded, both financially and professionally, and, even though I was living through tough times due to the environment created by the new faces of the drug-trafficking world, I tried to live a normal life.

In the midst of the fluctuating times, the new century arrived, bringing with it a new hope that maybe we could once again find ourselves together as a family. But the North American agencies would not rest and, under the guidance of Edward Kacerosky, they continued to strategize with the end goal of taking us before their justice system to pay for our crimes.

The altitude of a city like Bogotá began to affect my father's and uncle's health negatively. We moved heaven and hell to get them transferred to Valle del Cauca, but it had been impossible. Their permanence in Bogotá had been a direct order of the United States government, which had taken advantage of its close relationship with the general director of the National Police and controlled the transfer of all prisoners, including the Rodríguez brothers.

Fortunately, changes occurred, and they named two men who had collaborated with us in the war with Escobar to strategic positions. A general with whom we had a certain relationship was named as new director of the National Police, and the same thing had happened with Colonel Jaramillo, who was named as head of the Administrative Department of Security, DAS.

At the start of January, a man named Santiago, who had been my uncle's general doctor, went to La Picota to visit my father and uncle. He showed up as the personal doctor to the Pastrana household. It turns out that the new president needed a favor from the Rodríguez Orejuela brothers: something ironic, seeing as he had been the moral defender of the nation against the government of Ernesto Samper, and now he was asking drug traffickers for favors.

The honorable president needed to get an old ally of my

father's, a well-known money launderer in Valle del Cauca, to change his testimony against Álvaro Leyva Durán, a conservative politician, ex-minister, congressman, and party member. The president needed him in order to structure and enact a peace treaty with the FARC.

At first, his demeanor was aggressive and threatening, almost ordering them to comply. My father and uncle sent the doctor away with a simple phrase, "We do not comply to threats." The messenger returned the following week.

"What do you want in exchange for this favor?" asked the man in a calming tone.

My father and uncle asked to be moved to a prison in Valle del Cauca. This was the deal: the prison transfer in exchange for them getting Aparicio to change his testimony to their version. That is how the president was able to realize the peace accord with the guerrillas.

This is the truth behind their transfer, not what is said in the book, *El Cartel de los Sapos*, which claims that they were moved to Palmira because they told the authorities of a tunnel that Asprilla was planning on using to escape. My father and uncle are many, many things, but they are not rats; which is the reason that they are paying what is basically a life sentence, due to their code of silence, their "*omertá*."

With the president's blessing, and with no objection from the National Police or the DAS, they were moved to Palmira, an act that deeply worried the North American authorities as they saw this as a demonstration of the power still held by the Rodríguez Orejuela brothers.

Having them in Palmira made things a lot easier. The constant traveling to Bogotá was exhausting, economically and physically. It became a lot simpler to come to decisions regarding legal, financial, and business decisions. Whenever some misunderstanding happened with enemies, or a decision that could benefit all of the underground organizations needed to be made, I coordinated the visits to the prison with the help of Rasguno.

The extradition of Fabio Ochoa set off many alarms: it was a confirmation that sooner or later, we were headed in the same direction. In a meeting with my father in prison, my uncle said that any person in Colombia that did not think that extradition would happen to all of them was crazy; the North Americans and the Colombian government simply wanted to use Ochoa as a figurehead for what was to come. I believed that extradition should only be ruled for in a way that let all evidence be analyzed in Colombia, before the decision was made. And, only after the evidence allowed it, should anyone be extradited.

But that does not happen in Colombia, which is the reason that we had tried to make it not only an administrative process in the judicial and executive branches. Today, people are extradited from Colombia to whatever international court claims them. There is no guarantee for the prisoner that the evidence will be analyzed or that he will be allowed legal aid to defend himself; simply they are judged based on what they are accused of, not on whether the accusation has depth or not.

Because of the many things that had happened, I tried to turn myself into a ghost, to go about virtually unnoticed, aware that my attempted assassination and the constant mention of my name on the news had already caused irreparable damage. And, due to my conditions, I was a target for the Americans that saw in me the opportunity to build a bridge between what they wanted and had not been able to achieve: having Miguel Angel and Gilberto Jose Rodríguez Orejuela in a United States penitentiary.

There is no message clearer than this one: crime does not pay. Drug trafficking is a despicable act, as was stated by my cousin in an interview. Sadly, the entire family had to pay for it.

In the midst of all of these events, the Southern District of New York saw in me the perfect opportunity to gain protagonism in the community that was greatly focused on getting results in a war against crime, and especially against terrorism, in a post-9/11 climate. The justice system wanted to create a case where my name was involved. Through false information given by a witness, they initiated a case against me. Through the testimony of a paid-off witness, they falsely accused me of having participated in a criminal society and conspiring with Fernando Henao (the brother of Orlando Henao), when in reality, it was a well-known fact that the Henaos and the Rodríguezs were like the Capulets and the Montagues, rival families featured in Shakespeare's play *Romeo and Juliet*.

On December 22, an attorney that worked for a couple of offices with cases in the United States confirmed to me the details of the investigation being carried out against me. They painted me as an associate, co-author, and practically family member of Fernando Henao in a massive conspiracy to import tons of cocaine into the United States. The North Americans' mindset and their Calvinist ideas lead them to create precedents in order to maintain and sustain whatever case they want, as it was done with my family. The message to the rest of the world was clear: crime does not pay; the law, although harsh and sometimes unjust, is the law.

To my surprise, Fernando Henao, our former enemy, behaved integrally. He did not confirm any false accusations against me. I am confident that he did this because he knew that I was totally innocent. When I read the copies of the supposed emails that I had allegedly exchanged with the witness, it shocked me that the language used by both sides was quite vulgar. I felt offended not only because it was a gross fabrication but because it felt like an insult to my upbringing and my education. I must have learned something from my degree in Law from the University of San Buenaventura, or from the Master's I received from the Institute of Business in Madrid.

I was willing to submit myself to a lie detector test or any other way legally accepted to prove my innocence to the tribunal that was handling this case. My prosecutor knew this and in this my will was unbendable; plus, I could not let my supposed enemy down that, like a man, had upheld the truth above all.

Finally, after the long process in the United States, in which the District in New York fought for my custody so that it could apply a strategy of pressure to get my father and uncle extradited, the charges were dropped. A part of the evidence that they had against me was a recording of a conversation with their witness, where we discussed many illegal deals, but when they conducted a voice analysis, it was proven that the voice on the recording was not mine.

During the eighteen months that the investigation took place, I had to hide, doing things that I thought I had to do in order to clear my name, but it was in vain, because another investigation was started against me, this time in the district of Miami. Once I heard of this, I contacted a person I knew in DAS so that they could keep me updated on any warrants out for my arrest. The only thing is that this person never informed me, but, once again, my guardian angel intervened in my favor. An old ally in the war against Pablo Escobar was the person that told me about the multiple warrants out for my arrest, forcing me to begin this new stage in my life, when I was given no choice but to turn into a ghost.

CHAPTER 13

I have long reflected and internalized the political and judicial price of being the eldest son of Miguel Rodríguez. I have assumed this role due to my upbringing and my values, holding the reality that comes with this firmly in mind. Unfortunately, my father and uncle were unable to understand the true nature of the final chess game set by the United States. Yes, the US was not willing to forgive them for spearheading the world of drug trafficking, and much less was it willing to forgive the amount of power that they held and tried to utilize politically as they searched for a way out of their punishment, specifically through the election of a president and through Congress.

The social class that occupies the governing spots in Colombia was never going to allow two men, who were initially considered to be successful businessmen and were later considered to be the symbols of the international drug trade, to live out their lives as free men in the country. I always tried to get them to understand this, but my father and uncle, who had lost all sense of reality a long time before, were never able to consider what, to everyone else, was obvious. Even when they were in prison, facing the many difficulties of a maximum-security prison and the constant hounding by the American agencies, who monitored their every move, they refused to accept it.

The inclusion of our family on the Clinton List; the start of legal processes in different countries, where they had some kind of legal business; the processes against the majority of our family members, and businesses that provided for us; even the actions of forfeiture, were all demonstrations of the pressure and power of the American government. This plan was set in motion for years by the highest in power; the bourgeoisie, as soon as they felt safe, forgot about the many services my father and uncle had provided for them in the war against the most dangerous criminal in history and the only one that was able to bring them to their knees: Pablo Escobar.

My father and uncle, jailed inside the maximum-security prison in Palmira, were sure that they would get out of extradition with the help of some old friend. They tried to manage the time of their extradition, which had still not been formalized and that, according to them, was something that I had made up—hiring me a well-known attorney and professor from Bogotá, who boasted about his few victories and humored the wants of his client while wasting precious time and many opportunities to secure a better future for our family with the North American Department of Justice.

It is important to set a straight timeline and to clarify the authorities that asked for my extradition. It was the Southern District of New York that asked only for my extradition, and formalized it in July 2002. At that time, neither my father nor my uncle had been asked for by the United States, and they were close to being freed due to their sentences being completed. They were 100% sure that they would not be extradited since, according to them, they had committed no crime that merited extradition. Their warranty, according to them, was the Colombian Constitution.

In November 2002, my uncle was set free. A huge scandal erupted as no one in the entire country could believe that this decision had been taken; the entire world, in particular the US Department of Justice, believed that my uncle would never see the light of day as a free man in his entire life. Even though he was constantly monitored by police, I was able to meet with him on February 13, 2003, in a sector near Manizales; paradoxically, during that meeting, he was free and I was in hiding. He traveled to Armenia, and there, he changed vehicles so he could meet with me. The moment we met was emotional due to the current circumstances; we had lunch together and discussed our situation and the one of our family at length.

His perception was completely delusional. He, with his new-found freedom, had completely lost all sense of reality. When I told him that we should turn ourselves in to save not only our families, but some of our businesses as well, so that we could secure a financial future for us, he told me that he did not agree with me at all and told me I was being dramatic. According to him, the facts demonstrated this: he was free and my father would be free soon. He thought that they could solve my situation with time and by adopting a strategy to prove my innocence in New York.

I respected his opinion much, but sadly, he was not in the right. He kept sinking further and further into this delusion, and that is why he lost. He was convinced of his innocence, and underestimated his enemies in the north that would not rest until they saw him in a prison cell in the United States.

In March 2003, in an impressive operation coordinated by the DIJIN and the Colombian National Police, Gilberto was captured again. He was driving in a car through the streets of Cali when he was intercepted by five cars; twenty men spread out around him pointing weapons at him, and this number was not counting the ones that would soon show up. They drove him to the headquarters of the National Police so that they could process him, and, soon after, they transferred in a helicopter to La Picota in Bogotá.

While they were processing him in Cali, a captain of the DIJIN went up to an attorney, who was a family friend and worked with the DEA, to ask him about my status. In the end, he was able to convince him to get me to turn myself in so that I could make the lives of my family easier. They were all victims of countless searches as the authorities hunted for me. The actions of these policemen shamed the institution: they entered the homes of unarmed women and children to terrorize us into giving ourselves up. My wife and daughter had to endure the constant harassment of these "brave men."

Due to the proposal by Captain Mesa, who, ironically, finds

himself behind bars in the US due to accepting bribes from the organization led by Juan Carlos Ramírez, alias "El Chupeta," our friend kept meeting with him. The negotiators even went as far as setting a meeting up in Panama City to discuss the possibility of a negotiation and an eventual surrender, but it never actually happened. They wanted my father's head on a platter, which meant that they wanted me to testify against him. I told them no, and that, if that was the case, they had to come and find me.

Nevertheless, the messages from New York were clear: the materialization of extradition orders for Miguel and Gilberto Rodríguez were coming, and it was only a matter of time before they were there. The American authorities were willing to do anything in order to make sure that the Rodríguez brothers spent the rest of their lives in prison. The messages never stopped flowing—from them to me through my attorney and his colleague in Miami. Now, the cases were in two different jurisdictions and it was just a race against time.

The easiest way out for me would have been turning myself in and negotiating a deal, where the only beneficiary would have been me—maybe I wouldn't have had to spend a single day in prison, but this was not something I was willing to do to my family. Plus, I did not want the extradition of my father and uncle to be on my hands, even though some people may have wanted to blame me for their misfortunes, forgetting all the hurt they caused themselves.

The court in Miami asked for us to be turned over even without an order for extradition. In exchange for accepting drug-trafficking and money-laundering charges, they were willing to let us keep one of our businesses, with the condition that we turn in a significant sum of money to the United States. In this way, they would make sure to remove the entire family from the Clinton List, and would give me a ten-year sentence, with my father and uncle's sentences being twenty-five years for each. This was the most solid offer that we were able to get at any time, but it was impossible to agree on due to my uncle and my father, who continued to believe that they would be able to stay in Colombia.

On December 22, 2003, the media informed the entire country of the formal request for the extradition of Miguel and Gilberto Rodríguez, who were jailed in two different prisons in Colombia, caught up in a judicial fight for their freedom and for the negotiation of favorable terms.

From that moment on, my father and uncle started a campaign to persuade the entire political class to stop the extradition by influencing the Supreme Court and the president, who was in charge of signing off on all extraditions.

It was illogical to assume that a president that had already agreed to three extraditions would feel any kind of moral obligation for the Rodríguez brothers.

At the beginning of January 2004, Gilberto Rodríguez was extradited to the United States. I was hiding in one of the many homes I went through when I observed the horrific act on television. I felt a horrible pain in my heart over his fate; he had been like my second father. This moment represented the beginning of the end for the rest of our family.

I remember his final letter, asking me to stay hidden, promising that he would fight for our family and that they would win. In a certain manner, his extradition, although filled with sadness, signified the perfect chance to solve the entire family's problems and to finally be freed from our curse.

A number of months went by before they extradited my father. My uncle did not try to negotiate at all with the American authorities, knowing that my father was due to arrive at any moment, and that, together, they would be able to continue on with their long-standing strategy of facing everything united. The problem was that my uncle was still wrong because he believed that wasting time would make his strategy stronger, when in reality it did the exact opposite: the American authorities gathered more and more witnesses against them, and more members of the family began to be implicated.

March 11, 2005 was one of the saddest days in my life. My father was finally extradited to the United States. My uncle had not been wrong about that, and his brother was soon by his side. In a similar situation, I watched my father, like I had my uncle, be placed into a DEA plane headed straight for the US.

I tried to understand the range of feelings that I was experiencing. Anger, pain, sadness, despair; I knew that my father had lost this judicial war we had been waging for twenty years against the empire. I decided I had to turn myself into the United States justice system. With my father in prison, I felt that I had done my duty, as a son and a loyal member of the family, always keeping the collective in mind and putting everyone else above my individual needs.

The tears I shed while watching the images in front of me led me to re-evaluate my life, all over again; I retraced my entire life, what I had done, what I had not done, where I was, and where I was headed. Once again, I found myself having to find a way to save my family and to save myself in the best way possible, in the middle of the impossible, which was evading capture in Colombia.

I met with my siblings to analyze the possible strategies that we had to make in order to be ready when the time came to face what was coming, only this time we would not have my father's help. With my father and uncle extradited, we were at the mercy of the authorities that refused to leave us alone, and who continue to torture us today.

I was clear before the entire family. I told them that the moment had come when everyone needed to make their own decisions. I told them that my future looked a lot like what had just happened to my uncle and father, and they would have to think for themselves, never abandoning each other.

My uncle and, later, my father arrived directly at the Special Housing Unit, known as the SHU, in the Federal Correction Center in Miami.

It was obvious that communicating with them would become a lot more difficult; they were in another country, in one of the worst jails in the world, which meant that all kinds of communication had to be done through other people. As time went by, and we kept failing and searching for other ways out, we were forced to consider other alternatives, to have other expectations, so that we could arrive at some sort of possibility of building a life and of saving the rest of the family. We had to put our personal interests aside and make sure that the next generation did not have to suffer through what we had done: at least that's what I thought, but my father and uncle had a different idea in mind.

As destiny would have it, I accidentally received a letter that had been meant for my cousins. Because they knew that I was in hiding, they tried to keep the contents of the letter from my wife, where they outlined the strategy that they were going to use. In that letter, there was no trace of the promises they had made me through our attorney; it outlined their strategy for negotiation, which, in a few words, consisted in saving themselves, naively believing that they would get only a few years, and a strategy that, to mine and Maria's understanding, did not include me. That secret, their treason, was what set off my decision to turn myself into the United States.

After understanding that they were being informed more by wishful thinking than reason—with their hypothesis created based on ideas like that they would only serve fifteen years in prison, something that was simply not possible for the symbols of the international drug trade—I felt completely disappointed and let down by the people that I had been loyal to over everything.

In the midst of all the betrayal and the constant delays, during a moment of clarity and desperation, I remembered an old friend with whom I had some business back in the day, and a person that I knew had a US visa: Dr. Restrepo. I called him on the phone, and we met up to discuss a possible strategy to initiate negotiation talks with the American authorities.

Restrepo traveled to Miami with the power I gave him as my representative, through my signature and my fingerprint. He went straight to the federal building with every intention of reaching Edward Kacerosky, an expert on my family that had been in charge of persecuting us for over fourteen years. Kacerosky, obsessive and completely enamored with our case, had persecuted us mercilessly, and he did not rest until he had us behind bars in the States.

Once he was in the building, Restrepo informed the front desk of his intentions. He waited for over an hour before Edward Kacerosky appeared in the presence of a policeman and a DEA agent. As soon as they saw him, they asked him if he was William Rodríguez, and if he had gone there to turn himself in. After getting over the initial surprise and fear, he told them who he really was: the attorney representing William Rodríguez, not William Rodríguez himself.

Before beginning the official meeting, and due to the legal processes in the States, they needed the presence of an American lawyer that could represent and defend me, which is why they called Mr. Humberto Dominguez, who aided Restrepo through this first meeting to negotiate the terms of my surrender.

After this meeting, which Mr. Dominguez handled quite professionally, Restrepo scheduled a meeting with my wife and another attorney that I deeply trusted in Panama. The objective of this meeting was to learn the conditions that I wanted for my family and, logically, for me, in exchange for me surrendering to the United States' government; and, in that way, to prevent any of the many actions that are used in these scenarios to bring someone to justice.

A door was opening for the entire family and for me. I sent my father and uncle a letter outlining the economic and legal problems that were coming straight for us, and informing them of my position on the impending trial that was to take place the following year. Like always, they told me that I should wait; they believed that they would win on some motions that would guarantee that they would not be tried for crimes committed before 1997.

The position that they took is only understandable when we take into account the human condition and the immense power that they once possessed. Unfortunately, they were unable to understand the reality of the situation they were in, and, once again, they lost.

In the United States, punishments are given to make an example out of people, and this fact is widely known. My father and my uncle had no chance to win this, but they were unable to understand this, until history repeated itself once more. Even if they had managed to get all charges prior to 1997 dismissed, the case still had over forty witnesses, and they continued to get more.

The American attorney, Dominguez, was able to get a meeting with the prosecutors in charge of this case, who, understanding the situation that my family was in and that I was in, told me that I had the option of accepting the charges over drug trafficking: a move that meant the end of all hope for my father and uncle. My response was to send over a set of points, none irrational, that would benefit the rest of my family; the acceptance of those points was the only way that I would comply with their proposal.

I was not willing to sell out my dignity without getting at least some protections for my family members. It was a pragmatic deal, much in the spirit of the American philosophy. A good general knows when he must set aside his pride in order to evade worse consequences. In this case, if we went to court, many innocent family members would be dragged along with us. I anxiously waited to hear back from the American authorities; I felt like they were closing in on me, and that the time was about to run out.

CHAPTER 14

When I found out, in December 2001, that there was a process in New York, where I was being implicated for drug trafficking, I began to take some precautions. Through confidential information, I discovered that a group of eleven men from the DIJIN were gathering intelligence on me. I was also keeping an eye on them through my contacts, who had guaranteed that they would tell me as soon as they put out any warrants.

Twenty days before they formalized my arrest warrant, in the summer of 2002, I traveled to Cartagena to handle some business in relation to a case I was trying in this city. I decided to take advantage of the opportunity and stayed an extra week so that I could hang out with some friends in the beautiful city. My friends organized a night out with a group of women, who were from Cartagena, to an exclusive club. A particular woman, with a small frame, blonde hair, and honey eyes, caught my attention due to her quiet demeanor and the way that she analyzed everything around her. After sitting down at a table at the club, her silence turned into an extensive conversation that lasted practically all night. Her name was Regina. I took the precaution of keeping my identity concealed; she seemed to be so calm and content that I did not want to worry her.

When we left the club, we decided to go out on a boat the following morning. That night, after dropping her off at home, I considered that she might be the person I had been looking for. A friendly woman, who looked decent enough and had relatively average features, which made her presence quite easy to overlook yet vital.

The next day, we met up for the trip on the boat. We were seven people. I felt like, and I do not know why, it was a sort of goodbye; time kept rushing forward, and, with every second, I was getting closer to my true destiny. Nonetheless, we spent two days out at sea. On the trip, I had more time to talk with Regina. She told me that she was half Croatian, and that she had graduated as an economist. The side of her family that had migrated here was through her grandfather, who had fled to escape the Second World War, but had to make a mandatory stop in Santa Marta. They lived in the city for five years, just enough time for her grandfather to fall in love with the beautiful location. There, he met a beautiful woman from Cartagena and decided to remain in Colombia, forever. She also told me that her husband had been killed by paramilitary officers in that area, leaving her as a young and beautiful widow. It was a summary of her life that led me to understand the kind of strength one had to possess to deal with what she had been through, and to deal with the kind of stuff that I was about to be facing.

Engulfed by the grandeur of the night sky, lying down on the end of the small ship, staring at the stars that illustrated the enormity of the universe, I found the perfect moment to tell her a little more about who I really was. Before I did it, I wondered what reaction she might have: Would she be scared? Would she want to distance herself from me? Would she judge me? All of these scenarios went through my mind in a second, and I worried that it might hinder the ease with which we had been communicating until then.

As one can understand, she was surprised, but interested in learning more about my life. She even offered me her house in case I needed somewhere to hide. I thought it was just an empty offer, done out of courtesy.

The next day, already back in Cartagena, a friend of my father's informed me that a warrant had been issued for me. I panicked. I thought that we would be stopped as soon as we got to the harbor, and that I would be arrested. I told Regina, who remained calm. I decided to move through Barranquilla, hoping to evade the authorities and to have more time to understand what was actually happening.

While I waited for news, I decided to go to the movies. Halfway through the movie, I got a phone call from my father. He told me that there was no warrant for my arrest and asked me to return to Cali because he needed to talk to me.

Seeing as I had scheduled a trip with my wife and daughters to Santa Marta, I asked Maria to change the tickets to Barranquilla so we could travel together to Santa Marta. As the days went by, I was able to regain my cool and was able to enjoy the time away with my family before heading back to Cali.

My wife and daughters had another trip scheduled to Cancun for five days. After taking them to the airport, I drove to Palmira to speak with my father. It was July 14, 2002. We spoke about the grave situation that was closing in on us. He said, remaining forever optimistic, that things were going to change, but I knew that my fate had already been sealed. With tears in my eyes, I said goodbye to him as if it was the last time I would ever see him again. I will always remember that day.

My father's head was clouded: he was sure that the North American authorities would not ask for my extradition, still believing that Colombia's ruling class would stick by them and that they would be forgiven. He believed that we would simply go back to being businessmen with exemplary families.

The following Friday, I returned to Cartagena to deal with a situation regarding some property there. After that stressful, yet successful, negotiation, I decided that I would stay for the weekend so that I could enjoy what I consider to be one of the most beautiful cities in the world; plus, I wanted to see that reserved blonde that had captured my curiosity.

Saturday morning, I received a call from my secretary, who put me in contact with my father. He gave me the saddest news I have ever heard in my life: there was officially a warrant out for my arrest and extradition to the United States, so I had to flee.

Hearing this triggered in me a feeling of profound desperation similar to that portrayed by actors in horror films. I did not know what to do; I remembered my assassination attempt, where my life had flashed before my eyes. I got goosebumps up and down my skin; my soul hurt when I wondered what the future of my family would be and thought about the fact that I had lost the ability to make decisions on my own life. Processing this news was not easy; but, thanks to the strength of my spirit, I was able to subdue the pain and the worry.

After taking a shower, I got in contact with a personal assistant so that he could get me money and documents, and find me a way to communicate. I also reached out to a great friend of mine that has extensive knowledge of the rural areas in Colombia, who, by chance, was also in Cartagena. He told me the best routes that I could take in order to escape; this friend ended up being an avid man that knew everything, not only about Colombian geography, but also about how to travel under the radar.

The warrant that had been issued for my arrest only needed the smallest of formalities to come into effect. The operation for my capture and arrest was practically in motion. They had already studied my movements and my routines; they had been tracking me for six months. Curiously enough, there had been no record of my movements to Cartagena. According to their reports, I was on my way out of the country headed toward Argentina.

My assistant arrived in Cartagena on a plane. To avoid being followed, he bought the tickets in cash from Cali to Bogotá, and then, from Bogotá to Cartagena. He brought me travel documents, money, and the Avantel. Then, he returned to Cali, but when he was making his connection in Bogotá, a travel agent approached him and told him that a federal agent had asked him about him and his whereabouts, and, logically, he had been forced to comply. My assistant informed me of this news immediately, and I was forced to change my plans of traveling on a plane.

I called Regina. She was surprised that I had done this. To her, the nights we had spent discussing the depth of the universe were to remain in the past. She told me she had been dedicating her time to work and to her family; her father and mother took up a large portion of her time. Nonetheless, I could tell that hearing from me made her happy. I invited her to dinner. That same night, I told Regina about the situation I was in. I already felt like a fugitive. My confession had been so sincere and honest that she offered to come with me on my escape; she said she was the perfect person, as she would not get anyone's attention. It was true that the last thing I wanted to do was travel with a bunch of armed men.

My initial plan had been to hide without raising any suspicions. My idea was to go about unnoticed, but to do this, I needed to continue moving, pretending that I was on vacation, which meant I could not stay in the same place for too long.

The next day, I traveled toward Caldas. Regina stayed in Cartagena, coming up with places where I would be able to hide on the northern Colombian coast. In little time, we had forged a deep bond between us. She was like a god-sent person to me.

I got to Viejo Caldas. There, in a town called Santagueda, twenty minutes from Manizales, a difficult reunion with my family awaited me. We needed to plan for an unforeseeable future. One of the objectives of meeting with Maria was to organize a couple of things, like the way I was to communicate with my father so that we could coordinate how we were going to face this situation.

I created an email account that only my wife and I were to have access to. We would communicate through emails that we would never send; we would leave them as drafts. In the middle of this chase, I figured that was the best way of communicating without leaving behind a single trace. That same night, I wrote a letter for my father and handed it to my wife so she could give it to him; I wrote everything I was feeling.

The next day, Mr. Canaro and the attorney went straight to Cali. I had run into Canaro in Cartagena; he had showed me how to move through the country without being detected. In Cali, stimulated by the presence of my family, I began to analyze all my possibilities and consolidated my plans for hiding.

In Colombia, there are two ways to flee. One is to get a big security ring to prevent the authorities from getting close to the fugitive; this is the method used by most big criminals. For it to work, you must have a lot of money, and an extensive intelligence network; the danger comes from depending on the loyalty of too many people, and the result is usually not good for the person fleeing, as it is common that someone ends up betraying them.

The other way is a lot simpler and not as expensive. This second option was the one I adopted, and it gave me the desired results as I was never captured. Simply, it consisted of getting one person that would be in charge of booking all of the places where I would be staying in advance for periods of about two months: a beautiful yet simple woman that would not call too much attention to herself, and a friend, a man with a friendly presence and knowledge of the area.

The part regarding my identity was the first thing I dealt with. I had a fake ID made with someone who had a cousin that died but the death had never been reported.

"I need you to go and get me a Colombian passport with this ID," I told him. "I don't care how much it costs. It should be good because this person exists, he hasn't died, yet."

I completed my fake identity with a driver's license and a debit card.

Regina, elegant and attractive, was perfect for creating an image that did not raise any suspicions; she would act as my wife. Jose, a driver with a nice demeanor, accompanied me on my travels. Jairo, a friend that knew the areas well, would look for the properties where I stayed. El Viejo Caldas and the Caribbean coast would serve as the places that helped me conceal my feelings, worries, and hopes.

That is how I started this journey as a fugitive of the law. I was not being hunted due to my personal sins, but because of the ones committed by my uncle and father. The authorities knew that whoever captured me had the key to the kingdom.

My life turned into something that resembled the life of a rich, retired man. I dedicated all of my time to reading, playing chess, playing video games, browsing the Internet, and taking walks with Regina through the beautiful countryside. I hid in two places during those forty months: Cartagena, because Regina was familiar with the area and could access places easily, and Santagueda, where there were many country homes up for rent, and no one really knew who lived there or who was visiting. Plus, in this latter place, my friend Jairo had many friends and family that did not know of my situation or my identity and were a big help.

In order to get in contact with my wife or anyone in my family, I had to organize a tremendous logistical effort. Every time I saw Maria, we met in a different location. For example, a hair salon or at a cousin's house that she never visited, etc. We had three or four places picked where there was a landline; we did it this way because, if we used cellphones, the systems could recognize my voice. Weekly, I would leave the place I was staying in in Santagueda, I would go to Palestina, or I would stay close. Sometimes I went to Manizales to call her; I moved and, in this way, I could speak to her without being detected.

When I learned that they were offering 2 million dollars as a reward for my capture, I felt offended. Not because of the amount of money, but because of the injustice that was being committed. I thought about Jairo and Regina, the two people that were always with me. Would this money make them change their minds? It never happened. They never even considered it, which is why, today, I feel more than gratitude for them. I respect them and care for them deeply.

The days went by in between luxurious vacation homes, and I tried to appear to be leading a normal life; but, ultimately, the idea of facing my reality was always in the back of my mind. These were difficult times. I thought about other options, like traveling to Argentina. I knew that the authorities had already verified that I was not there, and it was unlikely that they would look for me there again.

Another option was to travel to Europe, to Croatia, and start a new life. Regina's family had some terrain there. I thought about it, I looked at it from all angles; it was a tough choice. If I chose this, I would have to forget about Maria and my daughters. I decided not to do that. What would my daughters think of me if I had made that decision?

In between one online chess match and another with people hundreds of miles away, all over the world, I imagined every possible scenario. In the end, every option ended up being a dead end.

As time went by, and I waited for a negotiation that would never come, I started to wonder if my father and uncle were handling things in a manner that would only benefit them. The more I thought about it, the less I could think but the more I could feel; after all, actions are what show our true intentions. I talked about this with Regina, who also could not see a good solution to this problem, and who was sure that she would not be able to be on the run for the rest of her life.

These reflections led me to make a transcendental decision that changed the direction of my life forever. I could either try to get my life back, the life that God had given me, or I could give it up and die an absent man with no way to turn back. The second option meant giving up the best years of my life, to give up being an attorney, to escape my reality for a world that would never feel real, to lose my home, my wife, and my daughters.

CHAPTER 15

Special Agent Kacerosky agreed to Maria's trip to the United States; in fact, he himself set everything up for her departure. He was anxious for her arrival; he knew I was the missing piece to his long-lasting puzzle.

I needed someone I could trust with my eyes closed and many say women have a sixth sense; therefore, I chose my wife as the negotiator of my possible surrender to the American justice system. I knew this decision would direct the course of my destiny. I needed to be sure the prosecutors of my case and Special Agent Kacerosky would live up to their word.

Once in Miami, Maria met with the special agent, who gave her a document outlining everything I had requested and—surprisingly—it was signed by all of the prosecutors related to my case. Throughout the remainder of the trip, my wife also met with multiple attorneys. Yet, my instinct told me I had to trust my defense to Humberto Dominguez, a well-known American jurist.

Upon Maria's arrival and after taking the necessary precautions since I was still a clear target to the authorities, my wife and I met on the outskirts of the city of Manizales. Maria told me she trusted both Kacerosky and the prosecutors. However, after reading the documents she'd brought, I decided I needed to negotiate myself. I needed to talk to Special Agent Kacerosky directly.

The charges I was being accused of were extremely delicate. I was charged with drug-trafficking conspiracy as I was being identified as a member of the Cali Cartel. The accusations were based on testimonies from witnesses who affirmed my father and my uncle had continued trafficking narcotics to the US from the penitentiary center La Picota, and declared I was the director of all operations. The indictment included seven or eight people.

Aside from my dad and his brother, it included two accountants, "Memo" Lara, and others who had nothing to do with us.

I immediately called Kacerosky from a public cabin in Manizales.

"Are you sure?" he asked.

"Yes, but are you sticking to your word?"

"You have my word."

"OK, I am in, let's coordinate the surrender."

"When do you want to proceed?"

"December 22."

We were toward the end of October at the time.

"Where?" he asked.

"Not in Colombia."

If I were to be captured in Colombia, I would have been sent to New York due to the case I had in the Southern District. In addition, I did not trust Colombians. I suggested Venezuela but he turned down my suggestion. He proposed Panama, a middle ground place I would be able to get to easier.

"You have to get to Panama, as there is someone I trust there," he said.

"OK, Panama it is …"

A couple of days later, I was able to meet with my siblings and cousins.

"These are the conditions of my surrender," I said. "All of you are included. There is no other way out; I am tired of waiting, and this is my decision."

"If you are sure they will validate your conditions, go for it," said my cousin Humberto. After hearing his words, I became at peace with myself; he had always been my rock in the most difficult moments.

Meanwhile, Regina was in Cartagena settling some things. The plan was for Regina to accompany me until my point of surrender. However, things got a little bit complicated when we saw each other. Regina did not support my decision. Her plans were different than mine. Perhaps she was hoping we could fly away together to Croatia, but I was tired of running and the only thing I wanted was to face my problems. Luckily, we were able to come to terms with our misunderstanding; I needed her. Regina was a citizen of Panama, the key to make it there.

Kacerosky changed the date of the surrender. He changed it from December 22 to in January. He recommended I spend the last holidays with my family.

I followed his advice. Just like old times, I spent Christmas and New Year's Eve with my wife and kids in the countryside. Yet, our holidays felt different this time around: cold and gloomy, with fear shaking the atmosphere.

Since the date of my surrender was soon approaching, I decided to tell my kids why their lives were about to take a 360-degree turn. "I am not a drug dealer; I have made some bad decisions but I never sent cocaine to the United States. My father and my uncle did and they are paying for it."

I promised them I was going to do everything in my power to get back home. I promised I would be back in five years—still I do not know why I said that number—but that is what I promised my daughters.

I said it in my testimony and until this day I can say it without hesitation: I never sent drugs to the United States. I helped a criminal organization buying consciences and running different companies. I have always wondered, why are banks never investigated? At a moment in time, my father had 3 million USD in overdrafts and not one single investigation was started.

After reading the indictment, I was shocked; I could not believe what I was being accused of. I was being charged as the successor to my father and uncle in operating the organization.

In October 2005, tired of running and without answers from my father, my uncle, and the lawyers, I shared with Humberto Dominguez my decision of surrendering myself to the American justice system.

One of the many precautions "Eddy"—I do not refer to him as

this in a loving way; this was just what everyone called him—took to keep this process going was the safety of my wife and daughters. He did not want to risk them suffering the same luck as the wife of Guillermo Pallomari, alias "El Chileno," assassination. I was falsely charged as the mastermind behind this crime. After my surrender, I was able to clarify I had nothing to do with this matter. Kacerosky wanted to be sure he could safely transport my wife and daughters the day after my surrender.

I called my team of operations to plan my trip to Panama; this trip was a total adventure. I had a Colombian passport with a Venezuelan visa. The plan was to fly from Caracas to Panama; the only problem was Interpol, as I was classified as one of the top priorities. I decided to back down from this plan. My other option was to travel from Capurganá, a hidden town with beautiful beaches from the Pacific Ocean that border with Panama. This option was definitely the safest. It was the only way I could escape customs.

I left the farmhouse toward Medellín with Regina and Jairo. At Olaya Herrera Airport, we rented a small plane and arrived to Capurganá. We got to a hotel, and just like any other tourists we asked what we needed to do to get to Panama. At that point, we faced the toughest part of the plan; we needed a special permit from customs.

Border control had augmented significantly since "Guerrilleros" were crossing the border to Panama for a "little escape." One of the requirements to cross was to send a copy of your passport to Bogotá, along with your fingerprints, in order to receive a permit within twenty-four hours. This was pretty much asking for a background check, and I was not in a position to take such a risk. I decided to abort this mission and we returned to Medellín.

I had to once again consider traveling to Panama via Venezuela. I flew to Cúcuta with Jairo on a 6 a.m. flight; I felt this was the best time to go unnoticed. Next, we would travel from Cúcuta to Caracas. Once in Cúcuta, Jairo and I took a taxi to cross the border and get to San Antonio Airport.

At this point of the trip, a miracle happened. At San Antonio Airport, there were many agents from the Venezuelan Police registering documents of the people migrating. In moments of great tension, it is when one needs to be calmer. Once the agent reviewing my passport started to question me, I thought, *This is it, this is the end.* I knew being captured in Venezuela would not only mean direct extradition to New York, but it would also mean my plan of surrendering myself for a better life for me and my family would have become an illusion. I prayed, "God, if you've allowed me to get this far, please do not abandon me now." At that moment, another agent came up to the agent reviewing my documentation and his attention was drawn away. That was my salvation; he then let me in. I cannot even begin to express the cold traveling through my body. I could not walk; I could not speak; yet I knew I needed to keep my composure.

Regina was waiting for me in Caracas, at the Sheraton Hotel. Regina was coming with me to Panama. The next day, we headed to the airport. I was lucky enough to make it to my destination without any sort of obstacles.

My wife and daughters were waiting for me in a hotel. I had already informed Eddy's agents I was in Panama. My surrender was now taking place on the 16th, not the 14th, in order for me to spend a little time with my family.

The time to say goodbye to Regina had come. I will always remember her as my guardian angel. I could not hold my tears back in such an emotional, time-ticking moment. This was a bittersweet goodbye, an end to an unconditional friendship.

Later, I headed to the mall connected to my family's hotel. I looked for the best way to enter the hotel and make it to their room. It was a special encounter, filled with emotions. It was then that I realized that the sacrifice I was about to make was all worth it. Having my family by my side after all we had been through seemed unreal. It was in this one special moment I remembered why I had run for forty months and why I had decided to surrender myself. I did not want to let them down. I would never have forgiven myself.

The next day, the FBI agent called my wife to coordinate her pick-up and arrival to the airport; the place where we were supposed to meet. However, the agent ignored that I was already with her. Once my three diamonds headed to the airport, I took a taxi and made it to the airport almost at the same time as them.

I introduced myself to the agent and, joking around while filled with nervousness, I told him I was backing out from my surrender. He said I was free to do it and that he would just simply say he had never seen me, sarcastically of course. We laughed as a signal of mutual understanding and he headed to the Police Department. We identified ourselves and I was immediately processed. They needed to verify I met all of the requirements to travel to the United States under FBI custody.

Once the verification process was over, I was taken to the VIP lounge of American Airlines. There, I met with two agents from the US Immigration and Customs Enforcement department sent by Eddy to travel with me to Miami.

It was time to say goodbye to my wife. As strong as ever, she gave me a comforting hug that gave me the strength I needed to finish what had just started. She gave me a soft kiss and as I looked into her eyes, I was able to see she was filled with hope. "See you soon," she said. "We will be together again in no time." She promised she would wait for my return to freedom along with my two kids.

I stepped inside the plane with the two agents from ICE. I had to sit in the middle of them. Up to this point, I was not being handcuffed. This made the trip a bit more bearable as I could keep some of my dignity. Many things crossed my mind throughout the three-hour plane ride to Miami. One of them was the fact that I was surrendering myself to the agent that was obsessed with his duty of justice and my biggest karma. However, I knew he was my only hope for a future. I gave up my freedom to the American justice system and I still hoped at that point that both my father and my uncle would do the same.

In Miami, at the end of the tunnel of the plane Edward

Kacerosky was awaiting. I remember his look as if it was yes-terday. He could not keep his eyes off of me. He looked at me the same way a hunter might look at his prey seconds before the kill. This was it. The end to a prosecution that lasted more than fifteen years. I was the missing piece to his puzzle. He knew he was seconds away from calling "checkmate" to the last chess game with the bosses of the Cali Cartel.

As I walked down the tunnel, I asked the agents which person was Kacerosky. They pointed toward the end of the hall and said, "Over there, the blond guy." We were finally face to face. I shook his hand and said:

"Hi! Mr. Kacerosky, I am William Rodríguez, I surrender myself to you … you won!"

You can watch William Rodríguez Abadía's interview on Shaun Attwood's YouTube channel by searching: Son of the Cali Cartel

OTHER CARTEL BOOKS BY GADFLY PRESS

The Cali Cartel: Beyond Narcos

By Shaun Attwood

An electrifying account of the Cali Cartel beyond its portrayal on Netflix.

From the ashes of Pablo Escobar's empire rose an even bigger and more malevolent cartel. A new breed of sophisticated mobsters became the kings of cocaine. Their leader was Gilberto Rodríguez Orejuela – known as the Chess Player due to his foresight and calculated cunning.

Gilberto and his terrifying brother, Miguel, ran a multi-billion-dollar drug empire like a corporation. They employed a politically astute brand of thuggery and spent $10 million to put a president in power. Although the godfathers from Cali preferred bribery over violence, their many loyal torturers and hit men were never idle.

Pablo Escobar's Story (4-book series)

By Shaun Attwood

"Finally, the definitive book about Escobar, original and up-to-date" – UNILAD

"The most comprehensive account ever written" – True Geordie

Pablo Escobar was a mama's boy who cherished his family and

sang in the shower, yet he bombed a passenger plane and formed a death squad that used genital electrocution.

Most Escobar biographies only provide a few pieces of the puzzle, but this action-packed 1000-page book reveals everything about the king of cocaine.

Mostly translated from Spanish, Part 1 contains stories untold in the English-speaking world, including:

The tragic death of his youngest brother Fernando.

The fate of his pregnant mistress.

The shocking details of his affair with a TV celebrity.

The presidential candidate who encouraged him to eliminate their rivals.

Pablo Escobar: Beyond Narcos

By Shaun Attwood

The mind-blowing true story of Pablo Escobar and the Medellín Cartel beyond their portrayal on Netflix.

Colombian drug lord Pablo Escobar was a devoted family man and a psychopathic killer; a terrible enemy, yet a wonderful friend. While donating millions to the poor, he bombed and tortured his enemies – some had their eyeballs removed with hot spoons. Through ruthless cunning and America's insatiable appetite for cocaine, he became a multi-billionaire, who lived in a \$100-million house with its own zoo.

Pablo Escobar: Beyond Narcos demolishes the standard good versus evil telling of his story. The authorities were not hunting Pablo down to stop his cocaine business. They were taking over it.

American Made: Who Killed Barry Seal? Pablo Escobar or George HW Bush

By Shaun Attwood

Set in a world where crime and government coexist, *American Made* is the jaw-dropping true story of CIA pilot Barry Seal that the Hollywood movie starring Tom Cruise is afraid to tell.

Barry Seal flew cocaine and weapons worth billions of dollars into and out of America in the 1980s. After he became a government informant, Pablo Escobar's Medellin Cartel offered a million for him alive and half a million dead. But his real trouble began after he threatened to expose the dirty dealings of George HW Bush.

American Made rips the roof off Bush and Clinton's complicity in cocaine trafficking in Mena, Arkansas.

"A conspiracy of the grandest magnitude." Congressman Bill Alexander on the Mena affair.

Printed in Great Britain
by Amazon